GOT A MINUTE?

The **9 Lessons** Every HR Professional Must Learn to Be Successful

By Dale J. Dwyer & Sheri A. Caldwell

Society for Human Resource Management
Alexandria, Virginia
www.shrm.org

Strategic Human Resource Management India
Mumbai, India
www.shrmindia.org

Society for Human Resource Management
Haidian District Beijing, China
www.shrm.org/cn

This publication is designed to provide accurate and authoritative information regarding the subject matter covered. It is sold with the understanding that neither the publisher nor the authors are engaged in rendering legal or other professional service. If legal advice or other expert assistance is required, the services of a competent, licensed professional should be sought. The federal and state laws discussed in this book are subject to frequent revision and interpretation by amendments or judicial revisions that may significantly affect employer or employee rights and obligations. Readers are encouraged to seek legal counsel regarding specific policies and practices in their organizations.

This book is published by the Society for Human Resource Management (SHRM®). The interpretations, conclusions, and recommendations in this book are those of the authors and do not necessarily represent those of the publisher.

The Society for Human Resource Management (SHRM) is the world's largest association devoted to human resource management. Representing more than 250,000 members in over 140 countries, the Society serves the needs of HR professionals and advances the interests of the HR profession. Founded in 1948, SHRM has more than 575 affiliated chapters within the United States and subsidiary offices in China and India. Visit SHRM Online at www.shrm.org.

Interior and Cover Design: Terry Biddle

Library of Congress Cataloging-in-Publication Data

Dwyer, Dale J., 1956-
  Got a minute? : the 9 lessons every HR professional must learn to be successful / Dale J. Dwyer and Sheri A. Caldwell.
      p. cm.
  Includes bibliographical references and index.
  ISBN 978-1-58644-198-2
1. Personnel management. I. Caldwell, Sheri A., 1966- II. Title.
  HF5549.D876 2010
  658.3--dc22
          2010013652   10-0122

GOT A
MINUTE?

Contents

Preface

Probably every one of you reading this book has experienced the following:

> *You're sitting in your office, in front of the computer. Stacks of paper, files, and forms sit on your credenza, your desk, and one of the side chairs. The door to your office is slightly ajar, and anyone passing by can see that you are there.*

> *Suddenly, a gentle knock, and a head appears in the doorway. "Got a minute?" You, of course, reply, "Sure. What's up?"*

Naturally, whatever it is never takes just a minute. Most employee issues involve a long story, complete with the details of what happened, what "he said," and what "she said." And, they want to tell it to you, because you are the human resource guru. It is you they wish to "run something by," or it is you from whom they seek an opinion about what should be done or whether they have already done the right thing and taken the correct action.

Your role is a complicated one. Sometimes you are father or mother confessor; sometimes you are like the Oracle at Delphi, dispensing advice and trying to predict the future. All of us who have been in human resources for any length of time know that our presence is important to managers and employees on a number of levels. For, in the greater scheme of things, we make a difference in our organizations in both personal and professional ways.

Some of the issues we deal with are tragic: a woman who has just discovered she has breast cancer, a man who fears his house might be taken from him because he can no longer afford his mortgage due to a cutback in his hours at work. We learn compassion and empathy through dealing with human beings who bring all of themselves — their gifts, as well as their brokenness — to work each day.

However, some of the issues with which we are presented are hilariously funny or eerily creepy. It is through these funny and weird stories that we often learn how to be more patient, attentive, and effective managers and HR professionals for all of our organizational members.

In this book, we want to share some of those stories with you. You may have experienced some of these situations yourself or, at the very least, some that are very similar. More than the laughter, though, we hope that you are able to learn some valuable lessons about how to handle situations, and we want to provide you resources that you can use to avoid some of the mistakes and omissions that occurred in the stories provided.

What This Book Is About

This is a book about mistakes, challenges, and the day-to-day frustrations faced by HR professionals in organizations everywhere. What you are about to read is real. We asked for your stories, and you gave them freely. The stories have been edited slightly for length, clarity, and style, but most remain exactly as they were sent to us. And, yes, there are some wild and weird ones![1]

Each chapter deals with a particular challenge faced by typical HR folks: substance abuse, chronic liars, culture clashes, sexual issues, invasion of privacy, policy violations, and much more. The stories are used as examples to demonstrate the issues or challenges, as well as to indicate mistakes that might have been made in handling them. We then take a look at what might have been the cause of those mistakes and what all of us can learn from them. Each chapter teaches us a lesson about how we can become better HR practitioners and managers.

Chapter 1 presents the unmistakable lesson that people say and do dumb things, so you need to accept that fact. However, we present some ways you can learn to spot those employees who are likely to create a myriad of headaches for you.

Chapter 2 highlights the importance of learning the norms of the organization so that you are able to implement changes more smoothly, while Chapter 3 teaches us that despite all the policies and rules in your organization, you can't enforce all of them fairly. In fact, some rules are structured to actually reward the very behavior you are trying to stop from occurring.

In Chapter 4 we cover some of the approaches that organizations use for training and rewarding employees. We point out some of the reasons they fail and how to insure that your organization's approach to training and recognition is more successful.

Chapter 5's lesson to "measure twice, cut once" applies to anything you attempt as an HR professional, because much of what you do can have lasting ramifications for you personally, as well as for the organization and its employees. Chapter 6 takes on the daunting task of identifying those who abuse alcohol and drugs, and further teaches you to employ the tests that help you do that more effectively.

Chapter 7 recognizes that relationships and untrustworthiness at work form the very basis of many of your HR problems and, as such, require some of your most difficult decisions and practices. Chapter 8 reminds us all that one of your greatest competencies as an HR professional is your ability to anticipate the worst that can happen and prepare for it while, at the same time, bringing out the best in people. Chapter 9 reminds you that it takes time to bring about change in your organization, as well as your own development. As you finish reading each chapter, we hope you will find some new ideas and approaches to dealing with the challenges you face every day. As a bonus, we provide you with resources that will make all of what you learn in the book easier to implement in your organization.

Who Should Read This Book

Whether you have been in human resources for a long time, or you are just beginning your career, this book is written for you — the practicing HR professional at any level. The insights presented here will help you to better understand how to prevent misunderstandings, clarify policies and practices, and make the most of the scarce resources we all face in our organizations.

Acknowledgments

No book is ever written alone, and this is no exception. Without the great stories all of you sent us, we couldn't have fashioned the examples that make the case for our points. We also wish to thank the Society for Human Resource Management (SHRM) for the smooth working relationships we've formed with the editorial and marketing staff. Finally, we'd like to thank our spouses, Kathy and Bill, for allowing us the quiet time to create and polish each chapter.

1

Accept That People Will Say (and Do) the Dumbest Things

I was interviewing a candidate for the entry-level construction position for which we hire about 30-40 people a month. As I was going over his application, I realized that he had not indicated a reason for leaving his most recent position. So, of course, I asked him. Here is the answer that I received: "Well, I was working in the ditch with another employee, and he was really getting on my nerves with his humming. I told him that if he didn't shut up, I was going to hit him over the head with the shovel and bury him. They fired me. But I think he just took it the wrong way."

***

One of the questions I ask at an interview is, "What is it about your favorite supervisor that made him or her your favorite?" One gentleman said, "He always covered for me." I then asked him, "What do you mean by that?"

"Well, when I was late or hung over he would come up with a good story to tell everyone."

***

One of my recruiters had called in sick and asked me if I could do a couple of interviews that they already had scheduled for the day. The candidates coming in were interviewing for a call center position. Right after lunch I was called to the reception area, because I had a candidate waiting for an interview. When I got to the lobby, I introduced myself and asked her to follow me to one of the interview rooms. We sat down and began the interview. Everything was going fine, and then I asked the question that I always asked every candidate at the end of the interview: "If you could change anything about yourself, what would you change?" I usually ask this question because people give answers that they do not realize would be harmful in an interview, such as "I wish I did not procrastinate as much" or "I wish I was more organized," and so on. This particular candidate looked at me and replied, "I would go and get implants so I could have a bigger rack." At first I just sat there stunned, and then I quickly opened the office door, thanked her for coming, and showed her out. Ever since that day, I have changed my question to "if you could change anything about yourself at work, what would you change?"

The hardest part of this whole experience was trying to keep from looking straight at her chest after her response and keeping my composure.

***

I represent a government entity that manages all criminal records, civil records, and court transactions. I once had a woman come to my office and ask for an application. She said she thought this would be a great place to work after having seen what our employees do in the court room on frequent occasions. To make conversation as she filled out the application, I asked what had brought her to the courtroom so frequently. She then proceeded to tell me that she had been charged with several criminal offences and thought that this would be a great place for her to work, since she already knew all about court.

***

When checking an applicant's background for a job at our local courthouse, I learned that the person had a warrant for her arrest for stealing at the bank from which she was just terminated. Imagine applying for a job at the courthouse when you have a warrant for your arrest!

***

I was working for a company that owns thousands of restaurants in a chain. I received a call about a night-shift manager at one of our stores who had done several odd things. First, she locked the doors to the restaurant prior to closing time. Second, she sat there in the lobby while customers banged on the doors from outside. Third, she was making out with her boyfriend in the lobby while customers stood outside. Fourth, she was walking around the store putting curses on the employees and telling them their eyes were going to bleed.

I traveled to the store and met with the manager to take her statement. She didn't deny anything, but it was her explanation that blew me away: "Well, you see, I'm a werewolf, and it was a full moon last night. I was starting to itch, and that's why this happened.

I stepped away from the table and called our corporate attorney who, upon hearing my story, put the telephone down and started laughing out loud. She confirmed that there was no legal protection for a werewolf. A witch, yes, she said, but not a werewolf.

I returned to the table and told the manager that I thought she should resign her employment at that time, or else risk being terminated for cause. She resigned without incident.

***

By now, you're probably thinking, "They made these up." But we didn't. You may even have had similar experiences or, at least, ones that are just as wacky. The question is not, "Why do candidates and employees say and do such things?" Rather, the question for HR professionals is, "How can I learn to spot the hidden signs and 'red flags' *before* we hire them?"

Many of us have been taught that we must carefully screen applicants' backgrounds for criminal records, substance abuse, poor attendance, substandard work performance, harassment complaints, and other potential problems in the workplace. We know that the "tests" for these potential performance problems must be job-related, and that the methods we use must be face-neutral, reliable, and valid. But how can you screen for anti-social behavior or for people who think they are werewolves?

Strong vs. Weak Situations

Thirty years ago, psychologist Walter Mischel described the way people decide how they should behave by describing the extent to which they pay attention to their immediate surroundings.[1] He found that when the situation was very clear about how someone should act, the person followed the situational cues very well and acted accordingly. For example, if a person came into the room you are in right now and shouted, "Fire!" most people in the room would clearly know to exit the room as quickly as they could without being told. In other words, Mischel called this a "strong" situation — that is, the situation itself strongly suggests how one should behave.

However, when the situation does not send clear messages about how to behave, or sends no messages at all, people tend to rely on their own personalities or innate tendencies to guide their behavior. Imagine that at some time in your life you have arrived at a party or gathering, only to find that you are under-dressed or overdressed in comparison with the other guests there. Or, you have entered the party, only to realize that you don't know anyone there, so you are not sure what appropriate conversations might be. These examples present what Mischel called "weak" situations: the situational cues are ambiguous, the behavioral options are many. In these situations people who are not sensitive to situational or social norms tend to show their true colors.

Interestingly, job interviews can be considered "weak" situations, particularly if candidates haven't interviewed in a while or are interviewing in a completely different organizational culture than they have been used to. Consider this story we received:

> *I am a recruiter for a national civil engineering firm. We had slated a job interview for a staff-level profes-sional for 7:00 a.m. and, due to traffic, I was late. Our candidate was early. Andrew, the office manager, was already hard at work, but was kind enough to meet and greet our candidate until I arrived. As soon as I entered the building I saw him. Our candidate was already chomping on a wad of gum, had his tie half undone, and had on a rather loud and colorful sports jacket. I*

immediately took our candidate to a conference room and offered him a drink. He requested a soda and proceeded to follow me to the vending machine. He saw that all we had were Pepsi products and voiced his concerns that we didn't have Coke products. We settled on a Pepsi. I have seen this on television, but never in person: the candidate popped open the soda and drank it down like a beer at a frat party. It was gone in 30 seconds. Once he finished, it was as if he had just consumed two high-energy drinks. He was all wound up. "So when do I start?" I proceeded to explain to him that we needed to complete the interview process before we could make any decisions on starting.

After interviewing him, I asked if he had any questions. "What are the bennies?" he asked. "Bennies?" I replied. "You know vacation, holiday pay, medical coverage?" I gave him a quick overview; however, in the middle of the dental coverage explanation, he interrupted and told me that it was great that we had dental, because he needed a filling and a loose tooth fixed.

Clearly, such behavior speaks to an inability to understand the situational context or, more likely, it reveals a complete disregard for the accepted norms of behavior for a professional context (and maybe *any* context). Fortunately, he wasn't hired.

Sometimes, however, the HR professional ignores clear signs of "social stupidity":

A well-respected vendor for our organization referred a potential job candidate to our VP of Sales. Both the VP and HR interviewed the candidate, and we subsequently hired him for an outside sales position. The new employee, who I'll call "Keith," worked for a week and then came to our corporate offices for orientation. The

*VP went on several sales calls with him during his first
week, and all seemed well.*

*Several seconds after meeting me for the first time, Keith
told me that I should expect a call from the hotel he
stayed in the night before "because, well, I didn't party
like a rock star, but nearly..." He told me that he was
really sorry and that it wouldn't happen again. I said,
"Good, it better not," and we proceeded into my office
and started the orientation. Five minutes into it, Keith
started fishing around in his briefcase. He pulled out a
coffee pack, the kind you get in hotel rooms, and interrupted me by holding it out and saying, "Here, I want
you to have this. You should try it. It's really good!" I
looked at him like he was nuts, but he simply said, "It's
OK, I have more! I stole a whole box of them off a house-
keeping cart."*

The company, unfortunately, did not read Keith's behavioral cues
very well either, because they hired him, only to terminate him
shortly afterward in light of additional evidence for his lack of
"social intelligence."

Finding Skeletons

It is likely that you may already do reference and background
checks and, if so, they are often revealing if the sources are
reliable ones. One problem, however, is that not every reference
given by the candidate will provide objective, accurate information. Additionally, some references will not give any information,
and not all organizations can afford extensive background investigations. So what can be done to find out some of these "hidden"
problems?

One way to accomplish this is to use the references given by
the candidate as network points. That is, use the contact given to

you as the primary reference to ask for another reference. Usually, if there are actual issues with a candidate, the primary reference will probably not provide adequate information, primarily because the candidate would not have provided the contact if he or she thought the reference would give out any negative information. However, contacting the reference and asking to be referred to another co-worker, customer, client, supervisor, etc., will take you one level deeper in your investigation. Another strategy is to contact someone that is not listed as a reference, but who you may know is affiliated with the organization or candidate (e.g., a board member you may know or a member of a professional organization, like the local SHRM chapter). Both of these approaches may provide more accurate information about the candidate's behavior, judgment, and skill sets.

One HR person we know who routinely hires retail sales clerks makes it a point of using a friend as a "secret shopper" at the store where someone she is considering hiring currently works. Her friend gives his impression on the sales clerk's demeanor, helpfulness, and product knowledge. It isn't necessarily fool-proof, but it is another source of information about a candidate's public image and sales potential.

Background checks have become particularly popular. However, there are very few truly free sources of public records. Moreover, employers have very limited access to such records, and this makes getting a clear picture of a candidate less reliable. Many employers do credit checks of potential employees, but research has shown very little connection between a person's credit history and subsequent job performance or on-the-job behaviors.[2] The job-relatedness of credit background checks is problematic, at best.

Interestingly, there are only four kinds of criminal records that belong to the free public access category: arrest records, criminal court records, corrections records, and state criminal repository records. In most states, there are very specific procedures that employers must follow in order to obtain and use these records. In addition, the Fair Credit Reporting Act (FCRA) is the federal law that governs how most background information on applicants and employees can be obtained and used.[3] The Federal Trade Commission (FTC), the agency that enforces the FCRA, has prepared a document that can clarify how to access information from these records. It is titled, *Notice to Users of Consumer Reports: Obligations of Users Under the FCRA*, and is available on the Internet.[4]

Using the Internet for Applicant Screening

With the increased availability of data on the Internet, it is no wonder that using a basic search engine like Google can provide some immediate knowledge about an applicant you may be considering. In addition, online background services that are reasonably priced, such as Intelius[5] and US Search,[6] can provide you with any amount of background information; however, as mentioned before, not all of it would be considered job-related, so be careful in using these services.

Some employers, and perhaps you are one, have begun to use sites like LinkedIn, Facebook, and Twitter to assess the social appropriateness and competency of candidates. Career-Builder's most recent survey, completed in June 2009 by Harris Interactive, has interesting statistics on the number of employers who report that they currently use social media sites, such as Facebook and LinkedIn, to research potential job candidates.[7] Of the 2,667 respondents to the 2009 survey, 45 percent reported that they used social media, which more than doubled from the 22 percent reported in the 2008 survey. An additional 11 percent reported that they planned to start using social media as a background check tool.

While it is not illegal to search these sites, be aware that use of the information to make a hiring decision can be a violation of the FCRA. For example, just like using a credit report to deny employment, the FCRA requires that before denying employment based on information gleaned from these sites, employers must verify the information and provide the applicant with an opportunity to dispute the accuracy of the information presented on the social media site. Moreover, the denial of employment based on the information must still be job-related. In addition, using information gleaned online about an applicant's age, marital status, race, religion, or disability could invite a discrimination lawsuit.

How to Discover Social Ineptitude in Candidates

By now you are probably wondering whether there is anything else human resources can do to spot these potential problems before they become a part of your organization and a headache for you. The bad news is that you probably can't avoid all of the problem employees. The good news is that you can identify some problematic personal characteristics, such as social ineptitude, by directly assessing the emotional intelligence (EI) of applicants.

The term "emotional intelligence" is generally credited to Peter Salovey and John D. Mayer, who described emotional intelligence as a "form of social intelligence that involves the ability to monitor one's own and others' feelings and emotions, to discriminate among them, and to use this information to guide one's thinking and action."[8]

Everyone has some level of emotional intelligence, just the way everyone has some level of general intelligence. Many organizations commonly use the Wechsler Intelligence Test[9] as a selection device to measure basic abilities and general intelligence; however, few use any method to measure the emotional intelligence of applicants, and those that do generally only use it for management positions. This is unfortunate, since one's ability to interact with others appropriately is generally an unstated requirement in almost all jobs.

At the very basic level of emotional intelligence is the ability to identify one's own emotions, feelings, and thoughts. At this level, though we may be aware of what we feel, we may not be aware of what others feel, nor may we be particularly adept at choosing appropriate behavioral expressions of our emotions. For example, in the first story, our construction worker felt angry at his co-worker's continual humming. This, in and of itself, isn't the central problem. The problem comes in his choice of expression that he'd like to "hit him over the head and bury him." In essence, by this comment he indicates a poor ability to process his emotions appropriately.

A second level allows us to use emotions to prioritize our thinking, directing our attention to information that helps us to solve problems and to consider multiple viewpoints and solutions. Our construction worker, had he possessed a bit more of this ability, might still have felt anger at his co-worker's humming, but he would have chosen, instead, to focus on the fact that he had to work with this individual. In other words, he would not have let anger determine his behavior. This would have allowed him to seek a different, more rational solution and, most likely, he would have kept his job.

At the highest level, we are able to analyze and regulate our emotions so that we do not demonstrate wild mood swings. By regulating and moderating our emotions, we are able to avoid repressing or exaggerating information we wish to convey. Our construction worker, at this level of emotional intelligence, would have been able to express his displeasure with his co-worker's humming constructively and calmly without making such a dramatic and unregulated emotional statement.

There are several instruments designed to reliably measure emotional intelligence, and we strongly suggest that human resources routinely include emotional-intelligence testing when hiring for any position that has requirements for effective communication and establishing or maintaining interpersonal relationships.[10]

Another Kind of Intelligence

Despite understanding the importance of emotional intelligence in predicting successful work interactions, there is another factor to consider: not all people have practical intelligence either. In other words, many applicants have "academic" intelligence (i.e., they can engage in tasks that are well-defined and that have "correct" answers or approaches), but not all applicants can solve problems that are poorly defined, for which there is incomplete information, or that have multiple solutions or methods for arriving at a solution. In some ways, this is similar to the definition of a "weak" situation discussed previously. Problem-solving and decision-making are a part of many jobs and, as such, require more than merely taking for granted that, because someone has a college degree or has work experience, they will be able to solve the kinds of problems faced in your organization.

Sometimes you can tell if someone has practical intelligence just by listening, as this recruiter discovered:

> *I was with a co-worker at a job fair. We were sitting at a booth with a table drape that had our company name and logo on it. On the table were a variety of giveaways, also with our company name and logo on them. My co-worker and I were wearing shirts with the company name and logo and also name badges with—yes—the company name and logo.*
>
> *We were each drinking a soda from Sonic.*
>
> *A candidate approached me and asked me if I was with Sonic and what positions we had open. I let her know that I was with my company, not Sonic. Then, I pro-*

*ceeded to tell her what positions we had open. She let
me know that she was not interested in the positions we
had available.*

*She then turned to my co-worker and said, "So, you are
with Sonic?"*

Needless to say, we didn't have any positions for her.

Another way to see if the applicant has practical intelligence
is to have the hiring managers in your organization generate a
list of problems that routinely occur and to let you know what
behaviors and outcomes are expected in managing or solving
these problems. This will allow you to construct behaviorally-
based interview questions that ask the candidates to reflect on
experiences they have had in managing or solving these types of
problems in the past. For example, if your organization has had
issues with customer retention because of how customer service
representatives handle product returns, an interview question,
such as "As a customer service representative in your previous
job, can you tell me about a product return that was particularly
difficult and how you ultimately handled it?" can help pinpoint
whether the candidate has the skills and practical intelligence
necessary to handle such problem returns in your organization.
Another great example is to ask the question, "Can you think
of a time when you put in extra effort to get the job done?" This
will help you assess the candidate's work ethic and what they
think constitutes "above and beyond" the boundaries of their
job.

One online resource that will help you create behaviorally
based interviews that are specific to the job in question is the
Interview Guide.[11] This program is based on the *O*NET Dic-
tionary of Occupational Titles* and contains over 900 jobs with
their associated tasks, knowledge, and skills. It is completely
customizable and provides applicant tracking and standardized

scoring capabilities, five modules of interviewer training, and statistical banding of job applicants into high and low bands. It is also reasonably priced.

Helpful Tips

1. Contact references and ask to be referred to another co-worker, customer, client, or supervisor. Consider also contacting people you know who may be familiar with the candidate's previous work history, but who are not listed as references.

2. If you use Internet or social media sites, make sure that you verify the information and provide the applicant with an opportunity to dispute the accuracy of the information. Consult the Fair Credit Reporting Act or an attorney if you are unsure about the legality of using online information for applicant screening.

3. Consider assessing candidates' emotional intelligence, particularly for jobs that require a good deal of interpersonal interaction (e.g., customer service reps, sales, receptionists, service personnel, healthcare workers, teachers, managers, and supervisors). Make sure you use a reliable, tested instrument.

4. Make sure that interviewers are trained in behavioral interviewing techniques, scoring, and the legal aspects of selection. A lot of problems with poor selection can be avoided by asking the right job-related questions.

Closing Thoughts

"Stupid" is not a protected group! You don't have to hire any employees who do not have the practical or social intelligence necessary to do the job you have open. Although it is sometimes difficult to detect in an interview who will be socially inept or might engage in problematic behavior at work, it is possible to incorporate behaviorally based interviews that get at common situations in your organization that the potential employee might face. In addition, incorporating emotional intelligence testing for those positions having a great deal of interpersonal contact will also help weed out many of the undesirable candidates. Improving the way reference checks are done and incorporating appropriate, job-related background checks will also help.

The bottom line is that nothing you will do will be an infallible solution, because people will continue to say and do the dumbest things. Consider, however, that these are the people that make your job interesting, even if they are challenging.

Norms Are Important for Leading and Managing Change

No two cultures — societal or organizational — are exactly alike. If you have ever traveled to other countries, you no doubt have observed widely different ways of eating, celebrating, and worshipping. In comparing societies across the globe, the acceptable norms for behavior, communication, and relationships vary as widely as their languages, foods, and religions. Visitors to different countries are often surprised by their observations and experiences in a new culture, because they are so different from their own.

When in Rome ...

Each summer for several years, Dale has spent three weeks teaching in south India. Although he has had students in the U.S. who were from India, and a good friend in graduate school who was Indian, he was not completely prepared for what he experienced on his first trip there. Besides language and food differences, which were expected and eagerly anticipated, he was most amazed by the traffic!

On narrow, two-lane roads are large commercial trucks, buses overflowing with riders, oxen pulling carts, two-wheeled motorbikes, passenger cars, donkeys, autorickshaws (small, three-seated taxis), bicycles, and pedestrians. There is constant, loud honking as all of these travelers attempt to navigate a dangerously narrow road, much like New York City or one of our large metropolitan cities.

The most fascinating part, however, is the difference between the traffic "culture" of the U.S. and India. In India, they accommodate each mode of transportation; in the U.S., in general, we are more concerned with our own progress and rudely cut off anyone who gets in our way. The common understanding in India that all must share the road, as well as how each traveler needs to be accommodated, allows for relatively smooth (albeit noisy) navigation for all. It is, in some way, an analogy for what we should be doing in our U.S. organizations.

This really is the essence of culture: a shared pattern of assumptions — a cultural paradigm — about how everyone in that culture sees the world and navigates through it together. But how do you learn what is acceptable in Rome if you are from India? That is the problem faced by every new member entering into a new cultural experience. In this regard, organizations are no different from civil societies. New members bring their own experiences, customs, and perceptions from their old culture into the new situation. In addition, the interpretation of the new culture becomes problematic, because new members see it with "old" eyes.

Many of you may have seen the popular movie, "Gung Ho!" It is a great example of a culture clash between an established, unionized U.S. organization that has been taken over in the mid-1980s by a Japanese automobile company. Both cultures experience discomfort with the "new" organization, particularly its management style and ways of working. They disagree, at first, about how to work and relate together. Primarily, of course, it was because they could not "see" through the other's lens. It was not until they faced a problem, together, that they were able to develop a shared reality about who they were as the "new" organization.

In any cultural experience, the language, rituals, celebrations, and stories convey a rich understanding of how systems and relationships operate. Culture, at its essence, is the set of shared assumptions that organizational members have created, developed, or discovered that helps them deal with the problems and issues facing the organization. As these assumptions get passed along to new members, a feeling of community is created that encourages employee commitment. In fact, the culture of a company can encourage others to want to join it, as demonstrated by this story:

> *In an effort to increase employee morale and employee engagement, as corporate HR manager, I suggested a "best costume" contest for all our employees on Halloween one year. As I went through the company promoting the Halloween dress-up day and soliciting employees to join the fun, I made a promise that I, too, would wear a costume on the approaching Halloween. Meanwhile, in an effort to recruit for a much-desired program manager/ engineer, I had scheduled the only day I could for this out-of-towner candidate on — you guessed it — Halloween. Imagine his surprise when I greeted him in a bright red devil's costume, complete with horns and tail! Nevertheless, he held his shock and amusement through the entire interview. Moreover, when it came to making him the offer, he accepted in spite of having to relocate his family. He told me he decided to take the job, in part, because he felt that we would be a "fun company to work for."*

This is an important point for HR folks, because they have the first chance to convey the culture of their organization to new members. However, a strong culture can also create feelings of isolation and exclusion for employees, clients, and customers who are unable to grasp the subtleties of the culture or who just do not "fit in." Even some things most of us take for granted can be different for those from other cultures. Consider this story we received:

> *I received a call from a manager indicating that he was receiving complaints about the condition of a bathroom after a certain individual would leave it. There would be water all over the floor — as if the toilet overflowed — there would be mucus splattered on the walls, the toilet seat would look rather dirty and wet, and the bathroom would smell awful. The manager and I talked about this, and he stated that he thought he knew what was going on. He believed that this individual was actually standing over the toilet to do his business, not understanding the proper 'Western' use of a restroom. The manager felt that the culture of this individual was the cause of this behavior and, if properly explained, the manager felt it would stop. A few days later the manager informed me that he had the conversation with the individual — can't imagine how that went — and that the bathroom has been clean ever since.*

In most of our organizations there are cultural norms about most behaviors, including language, dress, parking, work hours, relationships, and a host of other things. Part of HR's role is to convey those norms to new hires through direct conversations or by onboarding so that they feel included as part of the organizational community right from the beginning.

Organization-speak

One mainstay of a culture is its language and jargon — the specialized words and references used by the members of the culture that are often misunderstood by others who are not members of the culture. Jargon often gets in the way of clear communication, as this story points out:

> *I received a phone message from our CFO explaining that he was very concerned over a phone message that he had received and was not sure how to handle the situation, so he was forwarding the message to HR.*
>
> *The CFO had apparently asked an administrative employee to get pricing on a product from a vendor. The particular vendor he meant was a member of the credit union called a "SEG," which is short for Select Employee Group.*
>
> *In the phone message left on the CFO's voice mail, the administrative employee referred to this vendor as a "SEG." She kept explaining in the phone message that she was all for "SEGs," but didn't agree on getting business based on "SEGs."*
>
> *At first, I couldn't understand why the poor CFO was completely flustered by this phone message. I was finally able to decipher that he thought the employee was saying "SEX," and we all had a good laugh.*

Most organizations, industries, and professions have jargon. It is often what binds us together, provides us with shortcuts in oral and written communication, and generally defines that we are a member of the "in-group." As organizations try to broaden their inclusion of employees and customers, HR professionals are in a unique position to help translate the language of the organization and be sensitive to its effects on others.

We often take for granted that the written material we produce in our organizations can be understood by anyone who is literate. That, unfortunately, is not necessarily true, because of the jargon, shared understanding, and organization-specific assumptions that we make as we create it. In addition, the written material we provide says something important about our culture.

Take employee handbooks, for example. What does the following policy on bereavement leave say about the culture of this organization?

> *Staff members shall, upon request, be granted up to three (3) days annually of bereavement leave for the death of a parent, spouse, child, brother or sister, grandparents, grandparents-in-law, grandchild, son or daughter-in-law, mother-in-law, father-in-law, brother-in-law, sister-in-law, stepchildren, children-in-law, aunts, uncles, nieces, nephews, and first and second cousins. Other relationships are excluded unless there is a guardian relationship. Such leave is non-accumulative, and the total amount of bereavement leave will not exceed three days within any fiscal year. If additional days of absences are necessary, employees may request sick or annual leave, after providing an explanation of extenuating circumstances.*

Now compare this policy with the following treatment of an employee experiencing bereavement. This is an excerpt from a story that appeared in the *Boston Globe* in May 2007, about Jack Pichnarcik, whose 16-year-old son Mark died of leukemia. This is how Jack's boss, Brian Pomerleau, handled bereavement leave:

> *When Mark went into the hospital last November, Pomerleau told Jack to go be with his son, however long it was, and to be assured that he wouldn't miss a day of pay. He also slipped Jack a couple of thousand dollars over the next few months ... On the eve of Mark's death, Pomerleau quietly paid for all the funeral arrangements*

himself, then headed to Boston to tell the Pichnarciks that everything was ready and funded, no questions asked or money accepted.[1]

What differences would you expect in the culture of each organization? Which organization would YOU want to work for?

Employer Branding

In addition to policy statements that employees see and must abide by, written material that is used for marketing products and recruiting employees convey the culture of organizations, whether or not we intend for them to do so. Current thought, particularly regarding recruitment, is to create a "brand" so that potential applicants will consider the organization to be an employer of choice.

An employer brand represents the benefits that an employee might receive if they joined an organization. Just as product brands convey an image of the organization to customers, an employer brand conveys an organizational image to potential employees. It conveys what people might receive as a result of working for a particular employer.[2]

One way to cement your employer brand is to make use of technology. We have already noted the increased use of social media and websites, and there are several ways to convey the culture of your organization to prospective applicants using these exciting new tools.

First, consider whether a desirable applicant would rather read the static content on your website, or whether he or she would prefer to read a blog post or Twitterstream from the leader or employees in the area of the business they are considering. One great example of this is Zappos, the online shoe store, whose employees describe the culture in Tweets, and the CEO has a running Twitterstream.[3]

Second, consider using "job pods." These are video posts (aka podcasts) made by current employees describing the workplace culture, specific job openings, or career paths in their organizations.[4]

The bottom line is that you will benefit from conveying your organization's culture to prospective applicants. Those who actually apply for a job will have a better sense of whether they will fit with the company culture. Those who clearly see that there would be a poor person-organization fit will self-select out of the applicant pool. In addition, working with top management to "brand" your organization as a great place to work will help solidify your culture and create value for both current and future employees, making recruiting and onboarding much clearer and more pleasant for everyone involved.

Celebrate!

In addition to branding, there are many other ways that you can encourage a strong culture in your organization. For example, all societies use celebrations to reinforce their culture, cement their shared purpose, and reflect on their achievements. Organizations are no different. There are celebrations for birthdays and anniversaries. There are parties for holidays and retirements. And, for many organizations, celebration for professional and corporate achievements is a must.

For new members, celebrations say a great deal about what is valued in the organization and what is not valued. But they also convey who is "in" and who is "out" in the cultural pecking order. Are only sales goal achievements celebrated, rather than personal or professional goal achievements (e.g., college graduation, passing the CPA or PHR exam)? Does your organization celebrate National Customer Service Week (the first week in October), National Payroll Week (the first week in September), or do you typically celebrate only Administrative Professionals' Day? Do you celebrate the founding day of your organization?

All organizations can help cement their values by what they choose to support and celebrate. One story we heard highlighted a company's core value of "going above and beyond" by supporting an employee who went above and beyond his job duties to do what was right, rather than to do what was merely expedient:

> *In mid-May, "Sam" (not his real name) was driving his Dodge pickup down the road when a packing strap broke and five boxes of 1 1/2-inch screws flew out of his truck and fell all over the road. Sam stopped on the side of the highway and watched as dozens of cars hit the screws and suffered tire damage. He called to get his manager's approval, and then called the local Discount Tire Store and arranged for all the damaged tires to be replaced or repaired and billed to the company credit card.*

Clearly, Sam and his boss understood the culture of their organization and its value of "doing the right thing." As an HR professional, what celebrations can you devise that will reflect the values your organization truly wants to convey?

Story Time

Every organization has its stories — good, bad, scandalous, funny, and sad. These stories are the lifeblood of how the culture is passed from generation to generation of employees. In essence, they are the oral histories of the people, passed down by word-of-mouth, from the eyewitness accounts of past events, and can include folklore and myth, fact and fiction.

Consider how your own profession, human resources, is regarded in your organization. Sometimes, the stories that are told about the things we do frame the way employees, new and old, regard us. Like this story, for example, that illustrates how we are often perceived differently than we intend:

> *We had an employee who was in the midst of a performance improvement plan (PIP). In addition to her supervisor communicating with her on a regular basis, I also communicated with her periodically to see how she thought things were going. Of course, I thought I was being helpful, proactive, sensitive, and fostering credibility with this employee. ... You know, really showing her that I was committed to her success.*
>
> *While still in the midst of her PIP process, I had sent an email out to our entire employee population on some HR-related topic and signed it with my name and "Human Resources" underneath my name.*
>
> *Unfortunately, the employee's PIP was not successful, and we ultimately terminated her for poor performance. As part of our documentation, we were gathering some of her emails to support our case. One of the emails we came across was an email she sent to a co-worker in response to the email on the HR-related topic mentioned previously. Next to my signature line, "Human Resources," she typed the words, "more like Human Sacrifices!"*

Managers and top executives are often the most "storied" of the organization's culture. We received this story about a top HR executive in one organization that was passed along to others and is surely told to any prospective replacement:

> *My manager had some questions he wanted to go over with his boss, the VP of HR. He went in without an appointment, and got his head chewed off. At our next department meeting, he advised us all, "Do not, under any*

circumstance, go into _____'s office without an appoint-ment. I've had my a-- handed to me too many times for doing that. And another thing, if you see him walking around the department, don't just spontaneously try to corral him. Don't speak to him unless he says something to you first."

So, we followed my boss' directive. Seemed odd, though, that the VP of HR should be so averse to talking to peo-ple! After four years, mostly with his office door closed, he was reassigned and no longer has any direct reports.

The bottom line in storytelling is that you never know which story — heroic or career-busting, fiction or nonfiction — will be told to future generations of employees. As an HR practitioner, it is always wise to be the bearer of positive, laudable stories that teach new employees what the culture desires to pass on. For example, consider this story and what it might convey to employees:

The president of a large electronics firm was doing some photocopying after hours. He was wearing a white lab coat. A secretary who was closing up the laboratory saw him and asked accusingly, "Were you the one who left the lights and the copying machine on last night?"

"Uh. Well, I guess I did," was the reply.

"Don't you know that we have an energy-saving pro-gram in the company and that the president has asked us to be particularly careful about turning off lights and equipment?" she inquired almost scathingly.

"I'm very sorry, it won't happen again," returned the president.

The sequel to the story is that two days later the secretary passed the president, now dressed in a suit and wearing a nametag, when she visited the main office building. "Oh no," she thought, "I chewed out the company president!"

The most important point for those who told the story was not that the president had forgotten to follow his own energy-saving policy, but that he did not pull rank on the secretary. He felt bound by the rules he set like everyone else and he really seemed to believe in one of the "big ideas" at that company, namely, "We are a family here; we treat people with respect and as equals." [5]

In addition to the celebration of values and the stories shared around the organization, there are also symbols and artifacts that convey the organization's culture. These can be found in every nook and cranny, on every wall, and on every person in the organization.

What You See Is What You Get

The vast majority of the population is comprised of visual learners. That is, they learn by seeing, rather than by hearing or doing. Your organization's culture is also absorbed, often unconsciously, by what a new member actually sees for himself. Office décor, pictures and posters, logos, office arrangements, and modes of dress convey a "set design" for the organization's visual production. Go out and look at your reception area. Are there comfortable chairs, soft music, refreshments, and television? Or is the area devoid of comforts, a kind of "early 1960s doctor's office" décor, with year-old magazines and standard metal chairs?

Interestingly, one might think the comfortable reception area would be desirable, while the stark one would not be so desirable. However, the culture of the first may say to a visitor, "you are going to be waiting here a *long* time, so we wanted you to be distracted." Conversely, the other may convey that "we'll be with you so quickly, there won't be time to get comfortable, so don't mind the uncomfortable chairs."

The issue here is what you want to convey, as well as how it is seen by others. Offices with rat mazes of cubicles that separate employees from each other can convey a sense of isolation and exclusion, or they can communicate a sense of egalitarianism. Managers' offices that have real wood furniture tell a very different story than do those with metal desks and file cabinets. Again, we are not suggesting that one is better than another. Rather, the decision about the set design for your organization's culture should be consistent with that culture, or it will send mixed messages to employees about what is valued. Consider this rather innocuous behavior on the part of a manager and its effect on employees:

> *Our president kept a baseball bat in his office. People knew he was a baseball fan, so having a bat in his office was cool. However, one day, the president decided to take his bat with him on his walk through the building. He even swung the bat as he walked through the aisles! He made people feel very uncomfortable. I had a revolving door of employees after that incident. I tried to tell him what an uproar his actions caused, but all he said was that people were too uptight and should have known that it was all in fun.*

In addition to the décor of an organization, the clothes that employees wear also convey the culture of the organization. Does your company have a formal dress code or informal dress norms? Can you tell the difference between management and lower-level employees in your organization by the way each group dresses? Do you want there to be a distinction?

One organization we know of created a "casual Friday" policy, as I am sure many of you have done in your companies. Like most of you, the policy distinctly pointed out what the employees should *not* wear (e.g., tank tops, flip-flops, short-shorts), but did not specify what they should wear. One Friday, a young woman appeared at work in a flowing, gauzy dress under which she wore ... nothing! It never occurred to the HR manager to specify that employees should wear underwear on casual Friday.

In addition, the dress of the managers, including you, conveys much about the culture of the organization, as these two stories indicate:

> *Our company had a casual Friday policy, and the president of our company wore jeans and his favorite t-shirt along with shoes and no socks. We often involved him in interviews and thought that he should dress up a little more on Fridays when we had interviews, but he didn't. However, it actually helped us hire one candidate who told us after he was hired, "You know why I wanted to work here? I like how the president of the company dresses." He told us he had two offers, but he chose us because he liked our culture.*

***

> *In our company, we instituted a casual Friday policy in which the employees got to wear jeans; however, the president didn't own a pair of jeans. Each Friday the employees wore jeans, but not him. The employees began to tell each other that he obviously thought he was better than the common folk, otherwise he'd dress like everyone else, especially on Fridays. I delivered this news to the president, and while that was the farthest thought from his mind, he ended up buying a pair of jeans and started joining in on casual Fridays.*

Culture Orientation

Up to this point you are probably asking yourself, "All that's great, but how would a new employee learn about an organization's culture unless he or she spent time in it?" You would be correct in thinking that deep understanding of "the way things are done" around any organization does take some exposure to and experience with the organization. However, as HR professionals, we can also give new employees a leg up by introducing much of the accepted culture during an orientation session devoted to understanding what behavior is rewarded, punished, and celebrated.

For example, consider incorporating into the new employee orientation material a list of jargon and acronyms commonly used in your organization. Including a list of shorthand names for forms, too, surely would have helped this new hire:

> *During the first week of my new job as an HR rep in a hospital, I was asked several times about "the current STD." I was a bit embarrassed at first, so I didn't ask anyone what it meant (and hoped it didn't mean what I thought it did). It turns out it was a form that reported the comparison of monthly time-to-fill-position data with the hospital's benchmark STANDARD. Who would have known that?*

An organization's culture won't always be pleasant, because culture consists of the good, the bad, and the ugly of who we are as an organizational community. For example, consider the underlying culture of the organization in which this story occurred:

> *I had been working at a franchised Lebanese restaurant for almost two years. I started as a server, and after coming back from doing an internship in Washington, D.C., I moved up to an assistant manager. One of the*

partners bought out the other partner and brought in a new general manager. Those of us who had been there for a while had worked under a native Lebanese man before, but this time was different as he came in with an iron fist. He said that nothing was going to change and that he was not our boss but we were all part of a team. However, his actions did not coincide with his rhetoric. There were various altercations and outright arguments with employees. It was not a pleasant work environment.

One incident in particular highlighted one of the main problems: the lack of knowledge of what is appropriate in an American workplace. The new owner wanted to slash costs and, in doing so, would not allow us to turn the air conditioning on until five minutes before we opened. He also kept the temperature uncomfortably warm, which caused many of the servers to complain. One story I heard about was when Julie, one of the high school students that worked there, came to the new GM and told him it was unbearable. His response was "Well then, why don't you just take your shirt off."

An interesting fact was that he had been living in Boston as an owner/operator of another restaurant. I could not believe that he had been a business owner in this country for eight years and had not learned what you could and could not say.

I did not feel comfortable with the environment, so I quit and went to work at another restaurant, as did one of the best employees that worked there.

Losing a valued employee because of an unhealthy culture occurs frequently. The sad part is that many organizations are not even aware that the culture is often the culprit in employee turnover.

But now you know the awesome power of culture. Whether or not you know for sure why people leave your organization, it is part of your job to help manage the culture so that it isn't driving people away. And, to that end, we have some suggestions about how to incorporate a cultural orientation into what you now do for new employees as they begin at your company.

Helpful Tips

1. Conduct a cultural audit. We have made a template that you can modify to fit your organization.[6]

    a. Ask a variety of current employees and managers these questions: "What stories have you heard from others in this organization that best represents what ABC company stands for?" "What do we celebrate here that truly captures the best part of ABC?" "What language or jargon do we use here for which an outsider would have no clue about its meaning?"

    b. Walk around your organization and pretend you are a set designer for a movie or television show. What message(s) are conveyed by what you see (e.g., décor, behaviors, dress, etc.)? Are there competing messages, or does the "set" pretty much convey a similar overall message to you?

    c. From all the information you gather, make a list or a storyboard of your organization's culture. In your regular new employee orientation, invite the new employees to walk around for a day or two, and then to come back and share their perceptions of what they saw and heard. Then, share your storyboard. It will be instructional for all of you!

d. Conduct "stay interviews" after the initial 90-day intro-
ductory period. Ask if your organization or managers are
doing anything that would cause them to reconsider their
employment decision. And it doesn't have to stop there.
Conducting brief, periodic interviews will help you to
avoid culture-related turnover.

2. Incorporate Facebook and Twitter into your pre-orientation.
Invite new hires to link to current employees with whom they
will work. In that way, current employees can begin to share
information about the workplace, including dress codes or
norms, parking lot etiquette and protocol, lunch hour activities, and photographs of co-workers. Encourage current employees to reach out to the new hires by asking their opinions
and generally providing support and encouragement. You may
even want to start a new employee blog that provides important information about benefits, current events and programs,
product or service information, and messages from the boss.
You are only limited by your own creativity!

Closing Thoughts

The environment of your organization speaks volumes about the
values your organization holds dear. It provides the message to
new employees about how things are done, what is rewarded,
and who is "in" and who is "out" in the company. Whether it is
through jargon, stories, celebrations, or other means, organizations tend to create employees in their image. Sometimes this
results in strong, positive cultures and committed, loyal employees; other times, however, this results in negative cultures that
are exclusive and that drive high-performing, well-intentioned
employees out the door.

Helping to orient new employees in the positive aspects of
your culture should be part of any new employee orientation.
The "first impression" of the organization is a lasting one, and

it sends a signal for the attitudes, behaviors, and results the employee will be expected to adopt and be rewarded for adopting. Just remember that the point of any orientation is to speed up the awkwardness that comes with a new job, new culture, new products or services, and new co-workers. Finding new and creative ways of conveying those expectations will only help lessen discipline and turnover that is due to poor person-organization fit.

3   Some Rules Are Meant to Be Broken

In this chapter we will discuss the policies and rules that govern most employee behaviors at work. The problem for both employees and organizations is that some policies and rules have superseded good old common sense. Of course, you're probably saying to yourself, "But, employees don't always have common sense!" Not all of them do, that is true. Nevertheless, we believe that there are deeper reasons why employees violate the rules in your organization. Mainly, these reasons have more to do with (1) the perception of the relationship employees have with their employers and (2) the inadvertent reinforcement of the wrong behaviors.

Relationships Are the Key to Behavior at Work

Unfortunately, some organizations have gone to extremes to make sure that employee behaviors are controlled. There are rules about eating, drinking, smoking, driving, dating, dressing, parking, arriving at work, staying at work, leaving work, and a host of other things. What is missing, however, is the explicit expression of the values that govern our relationships with each other. All the rules, policies, and handbooks in the world cannot replace the importance of valuing our relationships at work. In many organizations today employees don't value the relationships they have with the owners and managers of the organizations in which they work. Likewise, employers convey through rules and policies, not to mention the message sent by downsizing and layoffs, that relationships with their employees in their organizations aren't as important as the "bottom line."

But it wasn't always that way. As Joseph Campbell remarked in his book and television series with Bill Moyer called *The Power of Myth*:

> *In the old days, when you came into a village, what you saw was the spires of the cathedral and the turrets of the castle, and it was from those two institutions, the church and the state, that all values came into the society. Now, when you drive into the city, you see the gleaming towers of commerce; within those towers aspirations are molded, ambitions acted out, neighborhoods formed, friendships and relationships built. A dense matrix of values grows up in those gleaming towers of commerce and makes their way into society at large.*[1]

The question for managers and, particularly, HR managers is, "what aspirations, ambitions, and relationships are we encouraging and building in our organizations?" In other words, what values are we placing on our employees' well-being and their importance in our business? More importantly, do our employees recognize the value we place on them?

Contract or Covenant?

Traditionally in organizations, especially in unionized organizations, the relationship between management and labor is defined by a contract. In a contract, either party can cry foul when something doesn't go as planned or when one party to the contract does not live up to its end of the bargain. Consequently, each can terminate the agreement as a violation of the signed contract. Employers contract with employees to provide their skills and talents; employees contract with employers to provide wages and benefits. When either the employer or the employee violates the contract, it typically ends the employer-employee relationship right then. At the very least, it damages the trustworthiness of the offending party.

In a covenant, the parties agree that the relationship will not always be fair — that sometimes, one or the other will have to give a bit more than the other. Marriages, for example, are both covenants *and* contracts. If a husband or a wife violates the marriage contract, each has the ability to end it contractually by divorce. However, marriage is also a covenant — an agreement that binds the parties together for all time. A solemn promise that no matter what happens, their relationship is more important than the trials and tribulations they will face, and that each will need to forgive the other many times. When two parties are in covenant together they are less likely to invoke any contractual boundaries.

Thus, the idea of a contract is, by its very nature, an economic relationship. For example, on the classifieds website Craigslist, a young woman wrote the following advertisement: "I'm a spectacularly beautiful 25-year-old girl. I'm articulate and classy. I'm looking to [marry] a guy who makes at least half a million a year. Where do you single rich men hang out?"[2]

In response, a man who claimed to meet her financial requirements said that from his perspective, her offer was a lousy business deal: "What you suggest is a simple trade: you bring your looks to the party, and I bring my money," he wrote. "But here's the rub: your looks will fade, but my money will continue to grow. So, in economic terms, you are a depreciating asset, and I am an earning asset." Rather harsh. However, in essence, she was turning marriage into an economic transaction — reducing what should be a sacred, covenantal relationship into nothing more than a contract.

Organizational covenants — often referred to as "psycho-logical contracts" — are not substantively different from marriage covenants. One of the major problems experienced by 21st century organizations and their employees is that the covenant has been broken. The covenant in an organization — the agreement that an employee's well-being is inextricably linked with the well-being and continuance of the organization, has slowly been undermined by downsizing, layoffs, scandal — and greed on the part of organizations. It has been violated by employees, too, in their own versions of "me-first" behaviors — sabotage, employee theft, chronic absenteeism, and laziness. With this degradation of the covenant between employers and their employees has come the need for greater control over the contractual language and consequences of rule and policy violations. Enter ... the employee handbook.

Failure to Comply Will Result In ...

Most of you reading this probably have an employee handbook, a union contract or, at the very least, a set of work rules that all employees must abide by. It is also likely that the handbook contains the consequences that will befall employees if they violate those rules. Some of them probably resemble the following:

The accumulation of twelve tardy behaviors in a "rolling" year (any consecutive twelve months) is grounds for employment termination. Disciplinary action, that may lead up to and include employment termination, may start when the sixth tardy in a three-month time period is recorded.

Disciplinary action, up to and including employment termination, will commence for the overuse of emergency personal time, when 56 hours of absences have been accumulated. The disciplinary action will consist of a written warning for the next eight hours missed, then a three-day suspension without pay for the next eight hours missed, followed by employment termination when an employee has used up any hours over 72.

Huh?

Do you have employees with limited education or limited literacy? Even if you do employ a number of college graduates, don't bet that they can all read and write at a college level. As teachers, we can tell you that the literacy level of new high school and college graduates is getting worse all the time! If you were to run a Flesch-Kincaid analysis[3] on the policy reproduced above, you would find that, in order to fully understand its meaning, one would need to have a grade level of 15 — in other words, three years of schooling beyond high school! For many of the positions in your organizations, this level of required education for employees is probably not realistic or even necessary. Yet, remember that your policies apply to all employees, whether or not they can read and understand them.

It is quite common for employee handbooks to be written far above the reading level of the very employees for whom they are written. Lawyers like to review handbooks and policies before they are released to employees. In fact, it is a good idea to have them do just that. Unfortunately, many lawyers often suggest revisions that include long, dry, and complicated wording. Although these statements help to provide "cover" for management decisions, they also tend to make the policy statement less clear for employees. As an HR practitioner, you need to be aware that including a lot of "legalese" in a handbook will not accomplish what the handbook primarily is designed to do: clearly communicate behavioral expectations to employees.

One organization we know of that installs auto glass has created a marvelous handbook that is funny, clear, and can be understood by most anyone. Here is a sample policy on substance abuse titled, "Stay Off the Grass (and I Don't Mean the Lawn)!"

> *We believe that people who decide to take illegal drugs or abuse alcohol are totally un-cool. Moreover, national statistics show that someone who abuses drugs or alcohol is 5 times more likely to get hurt at work. And, that person is 40% more likely to involve a coworker in the accident. So, our policy is to maintain a drug and alcohol-free environment. We also prohibit the sale or distribution of illegal drugs and other controlled substances.*

The Flesch-Kincaid reading level for this policy statement is ninth grade, still even a bit high for many workers, but a whole lot better than a 15. Newspapers are generally written around a sixth through eighth grade level, so this would be a good target for your policy statements, too.

Speaking of newspapers, the *Chicago Tribune* has a policy statement on email and computer use that is simple and easily understood at a third grade reading level:

> *It's good judgment not to put in writing what you don't want printed on the front page of a newspaper. Or posted on a website. Or heard on the news.*[4]

We suggest that you run readability statistics on your policies and see where they stand. Microsoft Word has an option in the spell-check function that can check documents for readability. Then revise your organization's handbook to get it to at least an eighth grade level, or lower, depending on your workforce demographics.

Less Is More

The Casual Day Task Force has now completed a 30-page manual titled "Relaxing Dress Without Relaxing Company Standards." A copy has been distributed to every employee. Please review the chapter "You Are What You Wear," and consult the "home casual" vs. "business casual" checklist before leaving for work each Friday. If you have doubts about the appropriateness of an item of clothing, contact your departmental representative before 7 a.m. on Friday.

Think the employees have read that 30-page manual? How many of them are likely to contact their departmental representative before 7:00 a.m. while they are trying to get the kids off to school or to a baby sitter, feed the dog, and get ready for work?

Most of the employee handbooks we've seen are certainly larger than thirty pages, and yours is likely to be long, too. It is always amusing when an organization gives a new employee the policy manual or handbook on the first day or two of work, tells them to read it, sign that they have read it, and then bring the signed form back. What percentage of new employees do you believe actually read it? Likely fewer than 10 percent read the entire handbook before signing the read/receipt form, although none of us will probably ever really know. Yet, managers smugly note that it doesn't matter; employees are still responsible for knowing and understanding what the handbook contains. However, some of the responsibility for making sure they know and understand falls on management, and as an HR professional, that probably means that *you* have the primary responsibility.

Probably some of you have your policies on an intranet so that employees who have access to computers can read them whenever they need clarification. However, not all employees in organizations have access to computers, and not all of them are computer-savvy enough to use them. For example, do temporary workers and contractors get a login to your intranet? What about fieldworkers and truck drivers? Do they have time to check the intranet news, or do they just use it to get their email? Are there some employees who only have network access to certain applications? Do some have Internet and intranet access blocked for some reason?

Of course, as the current Baby Boomer workforce (born between 1946 and 1964) retires, and Generation X (born between 1965 and 1976) and Generation Y or Millennial Generation (born between 1977 and 1994) begin to be the dominant workforce sector, the percentage of employees who are not facile with computers will diminish. Nevertheless, it pays to make sure that all persons who are covered by your work rules and policies have easy access to them.

Fun and Games with Handbooks

One approach to making sure that all employees understand work rules and policies is to schedule a discussion, perhaps at a brown bag lunch, about one policy each month. While you may be saying to yourself, "I don't have time for that," ask yourself this question: What percentage of your time is spent on interpreting and enforcing rules, dealing with discipline, and terminating employees because of policy and rule violations? We would bet it is at least 30 percent of your time — maybe higher. Using creative ways to talk about behavioral expectations (i.e., rules) will go much further in actually effecting changes in employee behavior than having an employee handbook that is four inches thick, replete with highly legal language.

One creative approach might be to have a contest for employees to rewrite a particular policy using as few words as possible. For example, let's consider the first half of the policy on tardiness we presented earlier. Here it is again in its original form:

> *The accumulation of twelve tardy behaviors in a "rolling" year (any consecutive twelve months) is grounds for employment termination. Disciplinary action, that may lead up to and include employment termination, may start when the sixth tardy in a three-month time period is recorded.*

Here it is rewritten in simpler language:

> *We realize that sometimes you can't always make it to work exactly on time. It is important for you to know, though, that you can be disciplined (or even fired) for being late too much. "Too much" is more than six (6) times in three (3) months. And if you are late twelve (12) times in one twelve-month time period, you might be fired.*

You could also challenge the artistic members of your organization to create a Haiku poem, a funny song, or a painting from a policy. You will be amazed at how employees will respond and, more importantly, engaging in such activities requires that the employees actually understand the policy and its implications for their behavior.

Reasonable or Unreasonable Rules?

By now you are probably wondering which rules should be in the employee handbook. Our answer is, "reasonable rules." But what is a reasonable rule?

A reasonable rule is one that has consensus across your entire organizational community (i.e., *all* members would agree that everyone should abide by it) and, therefore, none of the members would complain if it were enforced equally. However, therein lies the problem. Most rules are not enforced equally across the entire organization. For example, managers are usually not held to the same attendance standards as front-line workers; smokers are known to take longer breaks than non-smokers; employees without children are expected to stay later, work weekends, or work overtime while their peers with children are permitted to leave early for parent-teacher conferences, soccer games, or orthodontic appointments.

Current thinking is that workplaces should be "family friendly," and we don't disagree that all employees have a need to balance their work and non-work lives. For example, in the following story, it is clear that, for this fellow, this non-work situation was important enough to miss work:

> *An associate called in right before his shift and said he would not be in to work because his "mule" got loose! This was so incredible that no one believed him, not me and not his supervisor. But his wife called about three hours later and told me that he would be in about 1:00 p.m. as they had managed finally to corral the mule.*

How do we create rules and policies that take employees' work and non-work lives into account, no matter whether they are traditional ones or nontraditional ones? This is a challenge for HR professionals as they craft employee handbooks and seek buy-in from the entire community, from top managers to front-line employees.

It is as well to admit that workplace rules can never be enforced equally, but they should be enforced equitably. This means that if a rule unfairly targets a particular segment of the employee population (e.g., employees with children), then the rule should be examined with an eye toward restoring equity among groups of affected employees. Of course, sometimes a rule is applied equally across the board without much thought given to the result:

> *This story occurred at a seasonal food processing plant. Due to the seasonal nature of the business, there were some days when a large number of new hires were brought on board. As part of the onboarding process, the new hires were provided equipment such as rubber gloves, aprons, hearing protection and hairnets. The new-hire processing was a repetitive process for the HR staff and was handled the same for new male and female employees. The HR staff was under pressure to bring in new seasonal employees and get them processed as quickly as possible.*

> *As I toured the operations after several new hires were at their workstations, I noticed one of the new male workers having a problem. It seems his hairnet kept sliding over his forehead and ears. This gentleman had diligently followed the instruction to wear his hairnet at all times. I determined that this was not necessary in his case because he did not have any hair at all! I thanked him for his diligence and told him he was excused from the hairnet rule. When I met with the HR staff we all had a great laugh. The HR staff said that in the rush to get all new hires processed they had not recognized this gentleman's unique situation.*

Some rules in typical handbooks are antiquated or, at the very least, unreasonable for 21st century organizations. Often these unreasonable, out-of-date rules lead to higher costs and more problems than they actually solve, like this one from the Bay Area Rapid Transit in San Francisco:

Two employees are required for changing a seat cushion. A utility worker unfastens the snaps holding a seat cushion in place, and a journeyman mechanic adjusts screws fastening a seat into place.[5]

Unreasonable Rules Lead to Rule Abuse

The problem with "unreasonable" rules is that employees will always find ways around them. The following story is a great example of how employees deal with rules that make no sense to them or that cause them inconvenience:

In our building there is a door that is very convenient to enter for employees whose desks are near this door. A few months ago I noticed that by this door was a step that needed repairing. Being in charge of facilities, I presented the budget to our president with a dollar amount to fix the step. He said that rather than fix the step I should lock the door so no one could enter that way and, further, to convey a rule to that effect. He had decided that he didn't like employees entering our building via this door. I explained the convenience part, which he didn't care about. I also explained the fire safety concerns, so he agreed to allow people to leave that way, but they couldn't enter that way. He told me he saw people going out for smoke breaks and coming into work late that way, so he decided he was going to make it inconvenient for the employees and require that they enter and exit by the front entrance. I asked about the unsafe step, which was still an issue since he approved of people leaving that way, but he told me not to worry about it.

Of course, as soon as I announced the new rule, people were very upset. Even the managers of the two depart-

ments nearest the exit pleaded their cases asking to allow this door to be used for both in and out privileges. But, no, the president wouldn't allow it. So, instead of following the new, seemingly idiotic rule, the employees would just watch for each other or call from their cell phones for someone to let them inside. So, we now have several people being disturbed throughout the day to open this door, because people were determined to enter through the most convenient door, despite the new rule.

Or, consider the following story that highlights the ineffectiveness of rules, policies, and handbooks in the face of common practice:

I was the HR manager at a steel coating and processing facility. We were a 24/7, nonunion facility. On each shift we had an hourly engineer assigned to maintain the proper workings of the equipment, as well as to ensure their safe operation.

Our third-shift engineer was caught dozing off in a chair at the desk where he was supposed to be recording information. I witnessed him during a safety tour I had commenced around 6:00 a.m. I woke the employee up and summoned the shift supervisor who stammered a bit and then explained that sleeping a little bit on the third shift was not uncommon. In other words, this had been a common practice for this employee and others on third shift. I would also learn later that it was fairly common for the third-shift supervisor to also nap during the evening. What a great example to set!

I followed up by discussing this with our management team. After all, we had an employee handbook that clearly stated that sleeping on the job was a terminable

*offense. As a team we agreed that this was not appro-
priate and very unsafe. We realized we needed to reiter-
ate the "rules" and ask our supervisors to be responsible.
During our next plant-wide meeting, we explained that
while we may have been lax about sleeping at work in the
past, we would no longer tolerate it. We also posted this
policy on our bulletin boards and reminded employees
about our handbook.*

Interestingly, the above story goes on for some length describing how reiterating the "rules," placing responsibility on
the supervisors, and putting reminders about the policy on
bulletin boards did absolutely nothing to stop employees from
taking a snooze on third shift. In other words, while it is certainly reasonable to expect that employees are awake during their
working hours, merely having a rule about it did nothing to stop
the practice.

It seems that work rules and policies expand indeterminably
as employees find one way after another to skirt them. To us,
that says something about the culture of the organization and the
level of trust that resides in it. An organization's culture dictates
rules and norms for certain, expected behavior. In the case of
the steel coating facility, the culture of the organization accepted napping on third shift, even if the stated rule said otherwise.

Here is the rest of the story about the third-shift worker:

*The employee claimed that his wife had been ill. He had
taken her to the emergency room that day and, therefore, had not slept.*

*Within two months, this employee was caught sleeping
again, this time by our second-shift supervisor who was
filling in while his colleague was on vacation. When the
supervisor brought this to my attention, I suggested that
we needed to follow our policy and consider termina-*

tion. This employee had worked for the company for 18 years. We suspended him pending termination.

Even though we were nonunion, we allowed employees to bring another employee representative to any disciplinary hearing. The employee and his rep pleaded for his job. The employee claimed that his wife was terminally ill. But, he promised he would never fall asleep again. I asked whether he needed time off to care for his wife. He said "no"; he could not afford it.

What is the underlying issue here? Is it about sleeping on the job, or is it about trusting one's organization enough to come to the supervisor or to human resources when there is a problem that is affecting an employee's performance on the job? Is it about the process of discipline, or is it about providing an environment in which valuable employees can work out ways to attend to both their performance at work and their duties at home?

If your organization wants to rebuild the covenant with employees, it will need to start by assessing the rules and policies for which employee behaviors are held accountable. A great way to begin is to pull out the handbook and take a good look at what those rules and policies are really saying to employees. When the rules and policies are reasonable, the vast majority of employees will understand the rationale for them and, subsequently, agree with them. When they are unreasonable, employees will find ways to get around them.

The Dog Ate My Homework: Why Employees Lie About Tardiness and Absence

A candidate from a well-known construction company was attending an interview with a rival construction firm. During the interview a flustered worker burst into the room: "Whose Jaguar is that parked outside?" "That's my company car," replied the interviewee. The worker said, "I'm afraid a low loader has just dropped a full pallet of bricks on it."

The candidate, unfortunately, had to explain to his boss why he was at a competitor's premises despite having told his employer that he was at home sick. His defense was that he was just popping out to get some building materials for a job site. Needless to say it didn't wash. He lost his job and, worse yet, he didn't get the job at the rival firm either! I think it's fair to say that his interview performance might have been somewhat "biased" by the circumstances.

At some point, you will be confronted with an employee who lies, particularly about absence and lateness. According to a 2006 study of more than 2,500 workers by CareerBuilder.com, about 13 percent of American workers show up late for work at least once a week, and about 25 percent are late at least once a month. Of those numbers, one in five people said that they have made up lies to tell their boss about why they were late.[6]

The lies represent a range from failure to follow policies or rules to excessive tardiness, sickness, and theft. Of course, not all lies are harmful. We've probably all left home later than we should have for work at some point, but instead we blamed our tardiness on traffic. When this happens once in a great while, it is not such a big deal.

Our biggest headache, however, is with the chronic offenders who are constantly late, who routinely have flat tires or stomach flu, or for whom the alarm clock fails on a regular basis. We call this "serial lying."

I was working one morning and everyone was laughing and having a good time in the HR department. Many different people and managers at all levels of the organization were joining in on the fun. What everyone was so excited about was there was an employee in the receiving department that had called in sick the day before and got caught lying. As soon as he walked in the door he was asked to come to the HR office for a moment so they could speak with him. Little did he know that everyone was passing around the newspaper where there was a picture of him, a big smile on his face, fishing in the river the same day he had called in sick. He was fired on the spot, because absenteeism and made-up stories had been a big problem for a while with this guy.

Employees who lie generally start with "calling in sick" when they are not. This is such a common phenomenon that when we did a Google search for "sick day excuses," we came up with entire websites devoted to sample sick day excuses and protocol for calling in sick when you are not.[7] Here are a few of the oddest ones:

- *I can't come in today because the lady at the end of the road has just hung her wash out to dry, and I don't want to drive down the road, cause dust, so she'll have to do her wash again.*

- *I can't come to work as a skunk sprayed me last night.*

- *I was breaking the ice in my freezer with a knife and hit the whatchamicallit that gives the Freon to the freezer, and now my fridge is leaking Freon. As this is a hazardous substance, I have to stay home and wait for the HazChem people to arrive.*

There are websites that provide examples of excuses to give the boss, how to go about delivering a lie, and even a "BS" detector to see if the lie is credible! Isn't that an oxymoron?

But what is the real issue here?

Paid Time Off

Traditional policies encourage people to "use or lose" their sick time. In the spirit of generosity, some organizations allow sick time to be carried over for use in subsequent years or to be cashed in when the employee leaves or retires. One government worker shared with us that she was planning to retire in 2011, but that she would not have to work at all in 2010, because she had one year of accumulated sick time that she was planning to use before her official retirement date.

As employee absenteeism continues to rise, employers are also tightening their grip on employee sick days by decreasing the amount that can be rolled over from one year to the next. CCH, a provider of research products and software, conducted an Unscheduled Absence Survey that showed the number of employers who allow workers to carry over unused days into the following year has plunged from 51 percent in 2000 to 37 percent in 2004.[8]

The CCH survey also found that in 2004, employers offered significantly less sick time on average than in the previous year, but that the amount used by employees remained virtually unchanged from 2003. Companies granted an average of 6.9 sick days to employees in 2004 which, according to CCH, was down from 7.6 days in 2003. However, employees used 5.8 of those days in 2004, a slight increase from the 5.6 used in 2003.

In fact, CCH found that while people called in for a variety of reasons, only a third of the people calling in sick were actually ill. Ninety-one percent of organizations the CCH surveyed use some form of disciplinary action to control absenteeism, but the downside of such policies is that they also discourage employees from staying home when they are indeed sick.[9]

A solution? A paid-time-off (PTO) bank.

> *Absenteeism was at an all-time high, morale was low, and costs were up. Our average annual cost of last-minute no-shows was $750 per employee. We had to call in temporary help, because employees who called in sick were doing so at the last minute, and we couldn't plan for their absence. We had to set aside 5% of our budget to handle absenteeism. As the vice president of HR, I shared this information with our staff. When we had to cut back on our holiday party and bonus, I wanted them to see why. Once they better understood the impact to the organization and how that translated to their pocketbook, we began to work together to figure out a solution. We realized that all employees sometimes have things come up for which they need to miss work. However, the majority of these things were planned and for which the employer could get advance notice. We took a new approach. We tried to match our policies with our employees' actual needs. With a PTO bank, the time away is not differentiated and employees have more flexibility with and control over their time and how it is used. This was a win-win situation. In fact, subsequent employee satisfaction surveys showed a correlation between the new, more flexible policies and higher morale.*

Preventing Lies

Not that employers can prevent lies entirely, but here are some suggestions that will encourage employees to tell the truth more frequently.

- **Be direct.** Encourage your staff to be honest with you, to tell the truth, even on trivial issues. Only then will you be able to trust them on larger matters.

> *Jane, I have a hard time believing what you are telling me. You're chronically late and you continue to tell me that traffic was heavy (or you had another flat tire, or your alarm didn't go off, etc.). It's hard to believe that anyone can have that much bad luck. Now, please be honest with me. Tell me what's really going on. Perhaps together we can fix the problem. I want to help you but I need to know the truth.*

- When you suspect a lie, **investigate first.**

  Remember, there are two sides (sometimes three!) to every story. It may take time and resources, but it's important that you gather the facts and determine what action is necessary *before* disciplining the employee. If the offense is serious, get guidance from your legal department or an outside attorney.

> *I had a union employee come to me with a grievance, because he was devastated that he was disciplined for leaving a security gate open. His manager had come to me the previous day, and she told me that when she came into work, she noticed that the gate was not only unlocked but also left unopened. This had been an issue with the employee in the past, and he was the one assigned to late duty the previous night, so she wanted to write him up immediately. I was shocked that this had happened again, as I had talked to the employee about this before, but I agreed that he needed to be disciplined. When he came to me with the grievance, he asked one question: "Was anyone going to ask me what happened?" Whether or not he did it, he had a valid point. Both his*

manager and I jumped to conclusions assuming he was the one who had left the gate open. Had either one of us asked him, we would have found out that there was another side to the story. I jumped the gun. I didn't do my due diligence, and wrongfully accused and disciplined someone without having all the facts.

- Once you know the details, **prepare.**

Think through what you want to say to the employee and in what sequence. Practice by role playing. Anticipate the likely reactions and responses. Evaluate your own communication style, how you are perceived, and how you will react in the event of a challenge or emotional outburst. Knowing what you intend to cover in a face-to-face meeting and sticking to the agenda is much easier if you have planned in advance.

- **Confront the employee privately.**

Identify the problem as you understand it. Be brief but specific. Then offer the employee an opportunity to present the other side. There may be a factor you didn't know about that will help the two of you to solve a problem jointly. Refusing to listen just builds resentment and makes improvement difficult. Be fair to the employee. Consider his or her side of the story and any evidence submitted. Never criticize the individual, but rather *focus on the actual behavior.* Advise the employee of the consequences of his/her actions, whether it is a suspension or even a termination.

- **Document, document, document.**

There often is a misunderstanding about what and when to document. All disciplinary infractions should be recorded in some form. For minor, first-time offenses, write a note to remind yourself. This could be a verbal warning, but one that is documented, even though it may not require formal entry into a personnel file. If the problem recurs, or if it is a serious offense, be sure to formalize the process by having a neutral third party present and by having the employee sign that he or she has received the document.

- **Be confident** you made the right decision.

Lies are difficult to deal with. You are going to feel drained. Give yourself credit for having the courage to tackle a difficult situation. And remember: If you want to minimize your staff lying to you, never lie to them, and always deal with lies when they happen. As with anything, if it doesn't get addressed, it doesn't get better or go away; it just gets worse.

- **Don't forget to "think outside the box."**

As stated earlier with the PTO example, it is entirely possible that an organization's policy is encouraging the opposite behavior of what it desires. Re-examine every policy in place, at least every two years. Ask employees if there are issues or concerns with the policy. Does it work "against" employees or with them? Perhaps it is time to revamp rules and policies that have been in place for many years. Just because it used to work, doesn't mean that it's working today.

Learn to Play "Rule Roulette"

We are not suggesting that you throw out all the rules in your organization or that you eliminate your employee handbook. What we are suggesting is that you play "rule roulette" with your handbook. This requires an element of risk-taking to examine thoroughly each of your policies and look deeper into why they exist at all, as well as their relevance to current employees and situations.

Moreover, we suggest throwing out all the "silly" rules. What are the "silly" rules? They are the ones that keep everybody from doing what only a few people are going to do, and those people are going to do it anyway, despite the rule.

To begin, go through your entire handbook and ask these questions of each rule and policy:

1. What is the underlying problem that this rule is supposed to solve?

2. Does it continue to be a problem for many employees, even with the rule in place?

3. How much time do I spend dealing with the interpretation and enforcement of this rule?

4. Is there a better approach or a different way of dealing with the underlying problem?

While this may seem like a time-consuming approach, it will get at the fundamental reasons the rule exists. If the answers to these questions suggest revisions, we suggest creating a group of employees to examine the rules and suggest changes that all organizational members can accept. Involving employees at all levels in this group will create the buy-in and self-regulation needed to truly address the needs of the organization and its members. You will be better off in the end, and so will your employees.

A century ago, George Bernard Shaw observed,

> *The reasonable man adapts himself to the world; the unreasonable one persists in trying to adapt the world to himself. Therefore, all progress depends on the unreasonable man.*[10]

To paraphrase, reasonable HR departments create handbooks that look like every other organization's handbook (in fact, many guidelines say you should do this to avoid "recreating the wheel"). Their handbooks are primarily designed to protect them from lawsuits, even when the rules and policies are no longer able to solve the underlying problem for which they were originally created. The "unreasonable" HR professional persists in trying to find the policies that truly communicate the values that the organization wishes to promote. Remember, these values help attract, develop, and retain employees who understand why they are there and what their place in the organization means.

So be "unreasonable" in your approach to establishing and communicating rules and policies. If you can do that, it will be real progress toward building healthy and productive relationships with your employees.

What Are You Really Rewarding?

The second underlying reason that employees violate the rules and policies at work has to do with rewards. To demonstrate what we mean by this, we'll use an example of a departmental budget. Many of you are responsible for working within a budget; perhaps you are even responsible for creating your department's budget. Generally, budgets are annual documents, beginning on the first day of your organization's fiscal year and ending on the last day. For our example, let us say that your fiscal year begins on January 1 and ends on December 31.

If you have been fiscally responsible all year, e.g., buying supplies in bulk, curtailing unnecessary travel, and re-engineering some of the costlier processes in your department, you may have saved a substantial sum of money in your budget by the end of your fiscal year. So, on December 1, noticing that you will probably have several thousand dollars remaining, what do you do?

Our guess is that you look for ways to spend that money before December 31; otherwise, you will likely experience a reduction in next year's departmental budget. That is an example of rewarding the very behavior (spending) that organizations do *not* want and punishing the very behavior (saving) that they *do* want.

As a second example consider that, in a retail establishment, customer service is often proclaimed as the most important part of a front-line employee's job. Yet, these employees are generally paid a low, flat, hourly wage. Great customer service is seldom monetarily rewarded or even acknowledged by the boss. It's no wonder that retail sales associates are not motivated to provide great customer service, but they are often punished for not providing great customer service.

Organizational policies and rules create a number of situations that mirror the previous examples. Attendance policies are often among the most blatant offenders. When an attendance policy counts "times" rather than "days" absent, a five-day absence counts the same as one lasting two days. Such a policy actually rewards employees for staying home!

The following story is a perfect example of a systemic problem created by an attendance policy:

> *When I first began my HR career many, many years ago, I worked for a unionized manufacturing company that had, perhaps, the most horrid attendance control program known in the free world. If an employee worked the system right, a person could miss as many as 48 days a year and NOT GET DISCIPLINED! And then, once a person got into the disciplinary process, it was a six-step process, so employees had to work really hard to get fired.*

> *One employee, whose name was Jim, really knew how to work the system and was known for taking off Fridays and Mondays every other weekend, thereby avoiding disciplinary action.*

> *One time, he did get himself into a disciplinary situation and, while I was administering the discipline, I*

took advantage of the situation to ask him why, essentially, he worked only four days a week.

Very seriously, he looked me right in the eye and replied, "Because I haven't been able to figure out yet how to get by on three."

Behaviors of all types are difficult to change without changing an entire system. Health care in the United States, for example, tends to reward doctors monetarily for keeping patients under their care, rather than for keeping them well. Students are rewarded for high grades (e.g., by acceptance to graduate school or attainment of a job), rather than for the knowledge the grades are supposed to represent. Organizations promote the importance of teamwork, but most reward individual achievement. So, it is no wonder that many doctors run a lot of tests, students cheat on exams or plagiarize papers, and individual employees are not keen on working in teams. They all do what the system rewards them for doing.

Helpful Tips

Despite the fact that some rules and policies are necessary, we would like you to consider a few ideas to make sure that the ones you implement in your organization are reinforcing both the values and the behaviors you seek.

1. Analyze the readability of your policies. Rewrite any that are above an eighth grade reading level.

2. Play "Rule Roulette" with your employee handbook. Ask the (four) important questions to make sure the rules and policies are necessary and sufficient to solve the problem for which they were created.

3. Try some creative and fun ways to make sure your employees understand the important rules and policies. Make use of the

artistic talents and creativity of your employees to help clarify policies.

4. Make sure your rules and policies are rewarding the behavior(s) you want to continue. If a number of employees are in violation of a rule, or they are getting around it in some way, there is probably a systemic reason why. Work on figuring out what undesirable behavior(s) are actually being rewarded by the rule or policy. Then change them to reward the desirable behaviors.

Closing Thoughts

Human resources is usually the "keeper of the policies" in an organization. Often, HR professionals don't question the rules or policies, they generally just enforce them. However, you can have a tremendous impact on how employees view their relationships with management by considering the ramifications of your company's policies and rules on employee behaviors. Creating the trust that is necessary for employees and employers to rebuild the organizational covenant is based on equitable, fair treatment on both sides.

As Dr. Frank Crane, a noted 19th century Presbyterian minister, wrote:

> *You may be deceived if you trust too much, but you will live in torment if you do not trust enough.*[11]

By creating policies that reward the behavior you seek, management will come to realize that most employees do not come to work every day trying to do a poor job or cause problems. Rather, they do what they are rewarded for doing.

Don't Do What Doesn't Work

M ost managers sincerely believe they know what motivates employees to perform better, and they think they know how to make their organizations more effective and efficient. You've probably seen it play out in your own company with the creation of programs that focus on employee incentives and rewards, flexible work hours, telecommuting, merit pay, self-managed teams, and countless others. Or, perhaps your organization has sent employees to workshops or provided in-house training sessions to learn a "new, improved" method, such as lean manufacturing, Six Sigma, or *The Seven Habits of Highly Effective People*.

Why Didn't It Work?

Look in any company, and you are likely to see managers who adopt every newfangled approach to management that comes along. Although these managers often recognize that the new approach or program is not having the impact they would like it to have, they keep trying new approaches that take an inordinate amount of time and resources to implement. Moreover, with only 45 percent of workers reporting that they are satisfied with their jobs,[1] one would think that organizations would be more focused on finding out why the new approaches didn't work.

In this chapter we take a look at reasons why some programs and approaches to managing, developing, and rewarding people and their performance may not work. As an HR professional, you may be called upon to implement these programs and, unfortunately, to take the blame when they aren't successful. To that end, we'd like you to have some ammunition to respond to your manager when he or she says, "Let's do X."

Training Fads

We've all been there at a meeting when top management announces that, starting immediately, we are all going to implement a new approach, such as Total Quality Management, Balanced Scorecards, Re-engineering, Self-Managed Work Teams, or Six Sigma. It is not that these programs are bad ideas; rather, the unfortunate part is that they are often undertaken without a clear understanding of the organization's needs, or they are attempted by managers who don't fully understand how they fit into the "bigger picture" for the organization. The following story is a typical one in many organizations:

> At my former company, we always knew what book our president was reading. He would come to me, as the corporate trainer, and ask me to develop a program around the subject of his new reading. It started with Who Moved My Cheese?, then quickly moved to Stephen Covey's The Seven Habits of Highly Effective People. Both were actually very well-received by our associates; however, we didn't spend enough time on either initiative, so when he read Fish!, and we were asked to change our focus again to make people's day and to choose our attitude, it became one big joke. People began to ask what next month's training topic was going to be — in other words, what was the next "fad of the month." They lost interest in the sessions and became cynical, partly because they were being asked to switch gears so quickly. I could have possibly prevented this by asking more questions. Had I

known the root cause of why the president thought these programs would help our organization, I could have done some research to see if it was the right fit for us.

The previous story is a good example of how important it is to ask questions and to determine "fit" for a particular company. If a particular program seems to employees to be unnecessary, ineffective, or forced, it can cause confusion and even resentment. Diversity training is a great example. A study led by Alexandra Kalev, a sociologist at the University of Arizona, reviewed 30 years of data taken from 708 U.S. organizations.[2] She found that diversity training was often followed by a 7.5 percent *drop* in the number of women in management, and she concluded that forcing people to go through such training actually created a backlash against diversity. In other words, if diversity training is done merely to complete an item on a manager's to-do list, rather than to have useful, meaningful communication and inclusion, resentment builds against employees who are diverse. Conducting a needs assessment is always a good first step to determine the issue that the training or program should be focused on, why it is important to do it, and what the specific outcome goals might be.

Once you've determined the need and scope, it is then possible to evaluate programs that help address the need. Keep in mind that every organization has its own culture of how it likes to learn, and most prepackaged, off-the-shelf programs do not account for the specific context at all. As an analogy, think about all the infomercials for equipment, diets, or pills that you've seen on television that promise ripped abs, cardiovascular fitness, or maximum weight loss. Usually, in the small print at the end, almost all of these miracle products or programs say something like this: *Results are not typical. Part of a complete exercise and diet program. Results will vary based on individual factors.* In some ways, it is the same with off-the-shelf programs that promise higher sales, complete customer satisfaction, or an increase in productivity. Every organization must adapt a training program or management approach to its own culture and employees. You can help your managers see the importance of customization so that they do not spend a lot of money on a generic approach to a very organization-specific issue, because not every approach is applicable to every situation. Richard Hadden, co-author of *Contented Cows Give Better Milk*,[3] points to an example of how the Six Sigma quality improvement process was taken to the extreme at a company he once worked with. He writes, "Six Sigma became such a fad in that company that employees began to apply it to everything they did. They even tried to plan a luncheon conference by putting it through Six Sigma."[4] So before you adopt one of these "fads," make sure that you have done your homework. Identify the problem or issue the training or approach is supposed to address, and identify potential problems that might occur if it is adopted in your particular organization.

It is well-known that any initiative requires top leadership buy-in and commitment. Without commitment on the part of organizational leaders, most initiatives are doomed to fail. But how do you convince top managers that their presence and demonstrated commitment is crucial for the success of the initiative?

First, they should be among the first to be trained in the specific approach. Having the president and other top managers at each training session shows employees that management believes in the efficacy of the approach. A manager's presence also sends the message that learning and development is not just for lower-level managers and employees. If the manager's time is limited, try asking for key managers' commitment and participation times. Choose the times or events that have the greatest impact for employees, such as when there are practice sessions, training in use of tools (e.g., control charts, online assessments), or small group brainstorming. Avoid only the times when the training is just beginning or ending. That way, the manager is there when it is most apparent to employees that he or she really wants the approach to work.

Top managers must continually communicate the relevance of the approach to the organization's mission and goals. This helps employees see why they are being trained and shows them how they should be using the training in their own jobs. As with any training initiative, the transferability of training is essential.

Finally, leaders in the organization must be willing to hear from employees about the success or failure of the initiative, and they must hold all participants accountable to provide honest feedback. As an HR professional, your job is to help managers and employees communicate about "the good, the bad, and the ugly" of new programs and approaches. If everyone has to implement the new initiative, but also provides feedback about what is and isn't working, the entire organization is likely to be much more committed to its success.

Recognition

Our company had historically given gold pins for five-year anniversaries. Our industry had pretty high turn-over, in general, so not a lot of people got to five years. When I first started working in HR at my company, I decided to switch that to two years. I felt pretty good that we would be able to recognize far more people by distributing the gold pins earlier. However, when it came time to do the budget the following year, recognizing that we were cutting costs, I realized that I hadn't noticed one employee wearing a gold pin all year. I got out my list of those who received them, and I started to ask why they didn't wear them. I heard a myriad of reasons: "I forget to put it on," "It's at home ... somewhere," "It puts holes in my shirts," "No one else wears it."

Here I thought I was doing something special by allow-
ing the coveted gold pin to be given after two years of
service, when in fact, the gold pin wasn't coveted at all,
regardless of the number of years.

Management gurus talk constantly about the importance of recognition in motivating employees. Unfortunately, in many organizations, either managers don't recognize employees at all, or they do it badly. How much money has your organization spent on plaques, trophies, cups, pens, gift cards, award pins, and other trinkets that are supposed to reward and incent employees to keep their spirits up, solidify their organizational commitment, and increase or maintain performance? The question is, does it really work? Our guess is that it generally doesn't work for the people that you want to improve their commitment and performance, and the employees who have good performance would perform well whether they got a plaque or not.

Let us be clear; all of us need recognition. However, the problem for HR practitioners and managers lies in understanding that each of us differs in what is *meaningful* recognition. For some employees, public recognition is embarrassing. For others, a gift card to a restaurant or store seems trivial, but receiving a handwritten note from their boss is treasured. The point here is that managers need to know what is meaningful to each of their employees and reward them with what the employees would like, not what the managers think they would like.

Several years ago, we heard about a large-scale survey that was done about meaningful recognition. Almost 4,000 employees from all types of industries and organizations were asked to list the most meaningful recognition to them. Overwhelmingly, the respondents said that the following would indicate that their managers really valued them and their contributions:

1. Being invited to a meeting in which a significant issue or problem was being discussed.

2. Being invited by their immediate boss to lunch, just the two of them, to talk about their ideas, suggestions, and concerns.

3. Receiving a handwritten note from their boss that acknowledged their hard work or achievement in some way.

Notice that none of the three costs a lot of money, and none of them involves anyone but the employee's immediate boss. Again, the importance here is that each individual employee values recognition, but each employee has his or her own perception of what is meaningful. The more you can advise top managers in your organization to find out what is important to each direct report, the greater the impact of recognition on increasing motivation and performance. What's the best way for a manager to find out? Simply ask!

Employee-of-the-Month

Another problem with employee recognition is that sometimes it is done behind the scenes so that the person being recognized is not even aware of it. One story we were told had us both laughing:

> *I worked as a waitress in a large chain restaurant for about six months. One day in October I had an occasion to go into a back room that I hadn't been in since I was initially hired. It was a small office that the manager used when he wasn't out on the floor. I was leaving something on his desk when I happened to look on the wall behind it. Was I ever surprised when I saw a plaque on the wall with my name and "Employee of the Month" engraved on it. I apparently was the Employee of the Month ... two months before in August. Who knew?*

A lot of organizations have an "Employee of the Month," and we aren't suggesting this is all together a bad thing, *if* the criteria and nomination process are perceived to be valid and above-board. In other words, are the nominations only from external sources, like customers, or can they also come from inside the organization (e.g., peer employees or managers)? Do employees perceive the approach to be political, a kind of "If you nominate me, I'll nominate you"? Such aspects make "Employee of the Month" programs problematic, if they exist, in much the same way as the structured recognition programs we discussed earlier.

The criteria used are very important. It might be clear to employees that Susie should win because she has the superior performance. However, if she has consistently been a top performer and already received an "Employee of the Month" award, some managers might decide to "spread the wealth" and choose Jane who has never won. Unfortunately, this is de-motivating to all employees — Susie and Jane, included — because everyone knows who really deserves it. Thus, the intended purpose for recognition, i.e., increased motivation and commitment, is completely undermined.

Establishing a committee to determine the criteria for receiving an award such as "Employee-of-the-Month" helps clarify for everyone what is required. We are not suggesting, necessarily, that a committee choose the awardees, but having them participate in what it takes to get the award will help alleviate distrust in the process.

"I Want to Thank ..."

It is inevitable. A huge project is completed, on schedule, under budget, and exceeded the customer's expectations. At the celebration an executive gets up to thank all those involved. The executive calls out each person's name and asks him or her to stand or to come forward to receive an award. But there, in the crowd, is someone whose name isn't called. The person is insulted, and those who just seconds before were glowing from their accolades, are now upset with the executive (maybe even the entire company) for not being thorough and forgetting one of the most important people on the project. Not only does this have a detrimental effect on the person left out and the others involved in the project, but it ultimately affects the entire organization, as the following story demonstrates:

We had a formal recognition ceremony every year thanking all our sales associates for their work throughout the year. The assistant to the VP of Sales put together the program every year. She coordinated every detail of the event from the location and food to the program and awards. At the last event we had, the VP thanked practically everyone in the whole organization for their great work. He mentioned people in other departments who helped the sales team achieve their goals, and he even thanked the receptionist who was so polite to all the traveling employees and customers. His assistant was never mentioned. She got up after the thank you's and left the ceremony. It was pretty obvious that she stomped out, and people began to realize that she was never thanked. The VP sent her roses to apologize; however, she didn't come to work the next day and shortly thereafter, emailed her resignation. We never saw her again.

Likewise, there are situations just as de-motivating, such as when the "wrong" recipients get recognized:

Our company gives out "Atta Boy's" and "Atta Girl's" to employees who are recognized by an external customer. These are somewhat of a joke, because management often forgets to tell us that we've actually been recognized, even though the notice goes into a company newsletter. Therefore, we end up hearing it from whoever reads their newsletter first.

However, the stupidest one involved a customer service rep who was about to be terminated for poor performance. She was recognized by an external customer, and the customer's letter was published in the company newsletter, framed, and hung on our "Wall of Fame." In fact, the employee gave it a "high five" as she was being escorted from the building on her last day of employment.

These examples point to the problem that occurs when organizations structure recognition as a "program," rather than as an individual approach to increase the commitment and motivation of specific employees. Keep in mind that recognition "programs" almost never work; in fact, the more employees see recognition as a formal, structured program, the less likely they are to take recognition seriously. As a result, you'll spend a lot of money and get very little return on your investment, ultimately causing management to stop recognition completely for everyone.

Celebrations

Our VP of HR was responsible for setting up a holiday party for the employees in our very large organization. She went all out, having special effects built into the tables for very little money. In fact, she created a fantastic setting for a bargain. The entertainment was going to be great, the food fabulous. The buzz surrounding this party was incredible.

The night of the party, she went to the hotel to make sure everything would be perfect. She parked at the front of the hotel, got complimentary valet parking, and checked into her complimentary room. Then she went down to check out the ballroom for the extravaganza. Everything there was perfect.

What she didn't do was check the next ballroom over. The American Penile Surgeons Association was holding their convention and holiday party, and the entire crew for this very large organization was to be entertained by a 15-foot-high penis, with a great cut-a-way view that showed a plastic rod inserted.

The HR VP was absolutely livid. At the party, the rest of us left the room occasionally, mostly to laugh our brains out and to just stare in awe!

Holiday parties can certainly cause great angst for HR professionals. Sometimes the stress has to do with organizing the party itself, but often it has more to do with the appropriateness of the cultural dimensions of the holiday or the inappropriate behavior of some attendees (managers *and* employees).

Our boss (who nobody liked) was sad to announce to us that he would have to miss our holiday party because of a family obligation. During the party, we had a small gift exchange and almost every present had something to do with the boss and how much we hated him, such as his face on a dart board and "I Hate My Boss" coffee mugs. Halfway through the exchange, our boss walked in. His travel plans had changed.

Perhaps many of you have changed your "Christmas" party to a "Holiday" party to accommodate employees who are members of other faith traditions. Maybe some of you have experienced the feelings of dissonance that accompany having a holiday party at the end of December and laying off workers or cutting salaries shortly thereafter. Whatever the sources of stress, holiday parties are often not the successful celebrations organizations intend them to be.

So how do you organize a party that will have the right tone for your organization? Like our previous sections, we recommend that you focus on what the organization wishes to celebrate and be mindful of how it might be received. For example, if your organization has had a rough year economically and has had to make a lot of cuts in operational costs or employees, having an extravagant party with prime rib and champagne may cause employees to become resentful of the money being spent. On the other hand, a restrained gathering with cold cut sandwiches and beer or wine that focuses on a theme of "we have made it through this year together," may be just what employees need to remind them of the interdependence they all have with one another. Again, it will be impossible to please everyone, so focusing on the majority is the key.

Another money-related issue may plague holiday parties. Should you give holiday or end-of-the-year bonuses at a party? Absolutely not! Consider these next stories that point out the reasons why it is a bad idea to hand out money at a holiday party:

> *At our recent Christmas party, the boss gathered everyone together and gave an impassioned speech about the value of his employees. He then had his assistant give each of us an envelope. Ripping into our envelopes, we each learned our value — in the form of a single, crisp $10 bill.*

For most employees, receiving money at a holiday party can be embarrassing. But it may be even more embarrassing for the managers!

> *The worst holiday party I ever attended was actually quite nice until upper management handed out little or-*

naments containing cash. The company in question did not give out any Christmas bonuses. One employee who had been with the company five years (making her one of the senior employees, given the company's high turnover rate) was so happy about seeing the hundred-dollar bill in her little ornament that she yelled out the cash amount, which inspired other employees to open their ornaments. Unfortunately, the vast majority of the employees found a $5 bill tucked inside their ornaments. Fueled by cocktails and wine, the mood immediately changed from festive to hostile. The general opinion was that a $5 Christmas bonus was more insulting than no bonus at all.

Although these stories suggest that money should not be handed out during festivities, rewarding employees with monetary rewards is usually a good thing. Just keep in mind that money is a very personal matter and should be handled that way.

Picnics, Potlucks, and Pizza

Some organizations choose to schedule a company picnic instead of a formal celebration. It is a more informal way to show appreciation, usually because of the relaxation of the dress code, and because family members of the employees are often invited. Of course, picnics or other informal parties can also be problematic if the purpose for the picnic isn't clear or the scheduling poses inherent conflicts.

For some employees, picnics imply "family time," and they want their families to be invited; other employees are single and feel uncomfortable if the get-togethers imply a family affair. Sometimes picnics are scheduled on a non-workday so that it can be an all-day event; other times they are planned in the evening. But for many employees evening get-togethers can pose conflicts with non-work, family, or school activities. Some employers have opted to close the office for part of the day. And while many employees appreciate the time off, working spouses or partners and schoolchildren find getting off in the middle of the day to be problematic. As with everything, you can't please everyone, so why not ask employees what they want to do? You may be surprised at what they tell you they would like.

A simple way of acknowledging various events at work is to hold a potluck. Everyone has to eat, and with company budgets being so tight, why not ask everyone to bring in a dish to share to celebrate an occasion or just to celebrate your employees? It can even be a means of increasing everyone's understanding of diversity by asking employees to bring in a dish that they believe represents their heritage or has been in their family for generations.

Pizza parties are very popular. In fact, pizza is a fairly inexpensive party food, and many organizations use pizza as a reward for goal achievement or offer to throw a pizza party as an incentive. One nonprofit organization that we know of raised money by selling paper bats at Halloween. The agency involved a bank that had a number of branches to help with its fundraising efforts, and the bank pledged to match the funds raised in each of its branches. The agency was thrilled when it received an extra $2,500 from the bank at the conclusion of the fundraiser.

To spur employees to sell the $1.00 paper bats, the bank devised a contest for each of its branches and announced that it would award a pizza party to the branch that sold the most bats. This friendly contest brought the employees in each branch closer together and resulted in some very creative approaches to selling the bats, and then using them to decorate the walls and the front windows in each of the branches. Although the "winning" branch got the pizza party, the employees at each branch felt good about their participation in the friendly competition.

The upshot of parties, potlucks, pizza, and picnics is that they encourage and strengthen the bonds of belonging to a group. When you share food together, you also share life together.

Helpful Tips

- As an HR professional in your organization, one of your jobs is to advise top managers on what works and what doesn't in managing, developing, and rewarding employees. Gather data on employees' perceptions of training, new approaches to their jobs, and recognition and reward programs. Provide your managers with an analysis of why you believe something worked or something didn't work in reaching the goals or outcomes that top management has indicated the organization is trying to achieve.

- Analyze how you reward and incent employees in your organization. Determine what might be the most appropriate recognition for individual employees. Involve managers and peers if you don't know the employees that well, making sure to explain the importance and impact of individual recognition in increasing commitment and performance. Or, remember, it's just as easy to ask the employee what motivates him/her.

- Tie celebrations to something important in the company's culture such as team-building, goal achievement, or surviving another year successfully. That way you avoid any potential perceptions of bias due to religion, race, or other issues of protected group status, particularly with regard to holiday celebrations.

- Double check, even triple check, your thank-you list if you insist on naming individual contributors, or consider a more general thank you to all those involved.

Closing Thoughts

Managers, though well-intentioned, often do not think about why the training and rewards provided to employees don't work. In fact, too often managers blame the employees or, worse yet, you as the HR manager. But HR professionals can offer some great insight to top managers so that the money and time invested in training and rewards are not wasted. Do your homework, gather data, and make sure you understand what the organization is trying to accomplish with the training and recognition it offers. Once this is clear you will be in a much stronger position to suggest what *will* work, so that you can stop doing what doesn't work.

Measure Twice, Cut Once

Carpenters and builders have learned to avoid making mistakes the hard way, thereby ruining valuable and costly material. Cut the wood improperly, and the piece is unusable. So, the adage about measuring twice and cutting once plays in their heads every time they are about to rip into a new sheet of plywood or to position their saw on a 2x4. It is a constant reminder that they have one shot at getting it right, or it will cost time, money, and even reputation. Measuring twice means making sure that one has thought of all the things that could go wrong *before* acting or making a decision, and that maxim applies to human resource professionals as well.

While there is little research on the nature and cost of specific mistakes that HR practitioners make, a large number of the stories that we collected fell into this category. Hopefully the ones we'll share with you might make you think twice (literally).

"More Haste, Less Speed"

Many of the mistakes made by HR folks are due to a failure to clarify expectations about outcomes and processes. Not asking the right questions, not following the prescribed process, or failing to communicate clearly seem to be at the heart of the stories we read. In others, it was trying to rush to meet a deadline or to catch up. As Dale's grandmother used to say, "More haste, less speed." The more you rush, the more mistakes you are likely to make.

For example, in the following story, the HR person was clearly working during a very busy time of the year, she didn't have a lot of personal interaction with each candidate that would help her remember them, and she proceeded to circumvent the hiring protocol in order to wrap up the hire in what she thought was a timely manner. Unfortunately, as you will see, it did not go as everyone involved thought it should:

> I'm embarrassed to even share this story, but since it's anonymous, maybe someone can learn from my mistake. We were interviewing for a regional sales manager during the busiest time of the year. We had it down to our final two candidates. I had only met each of them once, but they had similar names. One's first name was William; the other one had Williams as his last name.

> A committee interviewed the candidates, and everyone liked the one with the last name Williams, but our CEO liked the other one whose first name was William. As I was heading to a meeting one day, the hiring manager asked me to extend the offer to Mr. William. He meant Bill, but he thought he was being funny calling him Mr. William, or "Mr. Bill." I heard Mr. Williams. I figured the CEO just went with his committee's decision to hire the one with the last name of Williams, instead of forcing the group to go with someone they didn't want (Bill).

> So, I proceeded to extend the offer to Mr. Williams. He was elated! He submitted his resignation immediately and said he could start the following Monday. He faxed me his acceptance letter, and I went to share the news with the hiring manager. I showed him the acceptance,

and he asked if it was a joke. I was confused, which he could tell, and he proceeded to tell me that it was the wrong guy. I turned beat red and thought my life would be over. He started laughing and said how glad he was that I went ahead and offered the job to the person we all wanted, but he said I was going to have to break the news to the CEO. The CEO wasn't so understanding. He told me to rescind the offer. I explained that he already resigned from his other job. He said that they couldn't have possibly replaced him yet, and they should just give him his job back.

As most HR practitioners know, it doesn't work that way. I explained that I had checked with the SHRM website online help, and while they can't offer legal advice, they felt like the candidate quit his job in good faith based on the offer I extended. So, I shared the legal concerns in writing. He checked with our attorney, who agreed with me (and SHRM), that we should honor the offer.

The CEO never let me live that down, and until this day, he'll ask if I hired anyone without his approval lately. Luckily, Mr. Williams ended up being the top regional sales manager in the nation in his first year and is on his way to doing the same this year.

Fortunately for this organization, the mistake actually turned out well. It makes you wonder, though, about their selection process if they were about to reject someone who, in his first year, became the top performer in the country!

A similar story ended quite differently:

Did you ever offer the wrong candidate the job? I did. We had narrowed the search to two candidates, and I mistakenly offered the position to the one we decided not

to hire. The hiring manager reminded me of our deci-
sion the next day. Then he said, "Boy, this is embarrass-
ing. How are you going to explain this?" What could I
do? I called the candidate back, apologized profusely for
my error, and prayed that our paths would never cross
again.

How did these mistakes really happen? Clearly, being
extremely busy often makes us overlook important details.
Sometimes we try to take short cuts or to rush in order to get our
work done by a deadline that is either self-set or set by others.
However, these stories also point out the importance of following
the agreed-upon process, step by step. By making an offer to a
candidate without first having an offer letter signed by the hiring
authority, the HR managers were able to circumvent the regular
process.

However, a more egregious error seems evident in each of
these stories as well. Both of these incidents suggest that there
was little documentation to refer to as the HR practitioner began
the process of making job offers. Without signed offer letters,
selection scores, or other indicators, the HR professional had
only his or her memory and perception to rely upon. And, as we
saw, neither was accurate.

Each of these hiring scenarios could have turned out to be a
costly mistake, both legally and from a public relations perspective. Taking advantage of using SHRM resources helped the first
HR manager answer her ultimate problem of whether the offer
could or should be rescinded. However, for legal matters, it is
worthwhile to have an attorney, as he or she can help keep you
legally on the high road, and most CEOs are not likely to challenge their attorney's advice.

Too Many Silly Mistakes Erode Trust

As we saw in Chapter 3, trust is a prerequisite for establishing and maintaining relationships. Trust can be undermined by malicious intent, but it can also be undermined by incompetence. When a manager is inconsistent in following process or doesn't communicate clearly about expectations, employees begin to see the manager as incompetent.

The following story shows the importance of clarity and consistency in all our HR practices:

> *The hiring manager wanted to hire a creative director. At our company, the word "director" was a coveted title. In this case, however, it was not really indicative of the level of this particular position. So, I talked to the candidate and explained some of the politics surrounding that title, and I extended the offer as a "creative manager."*
>
> *When we announced the new hire, people were very pleased to have a fellow manager. That is until they saw her business card. Her manager ordered her business cards with the title of "creative director."*
>
> *Needless to say, this created a revolving door at my office. People were upset that we introduced her as creative manager, but we put creative director on her business cards. I explained what had happened, but many thought we were trying to be deceptive. Those that didn't share this belief just thought we were incompetent and couldn't get the title right.*

Like the mistakes highlighted in the earlier stories, this is another example of poor communication between the HR department and the hiring manager. However, this HR manager learned a very valuable lesson about involving the hiring manager in the process:

> *I learned the importance of getting the manager on the same page as me before the offer is made. We started making the offers together, in fact. It actually worked out quite well, because often the candidate would ask something that only the hiring manager would know. Their questions could get answered immediately without me having to go ask the hiring manager and then call the candidate back.*

In addition, this manager also learned an important lesson about restructuring a process and refining how she approached her job:

> *We decided to centralize the ordering of business cards. The administrative assistant in HR was the only one who was allowed to order cards as a result of this mistake. She was able to match titles of offer letters to job descriptions. We ended up catching several errors, even simple ones like how the person wanted his or her name listed on the business card. This also generated some cost savings for us; because we were ordering more cards at one time, instead of one small order here and there, we were able to take advantage of the discounted bulk rate.*

The process of ordering business cards not only helped the company be more consistent and avoid errors, but it ultimately helped save money.

Had the above process been in place at the company below, they too could have saved time, money, and credibility:

> *The HR assistant at our company shared an office with the sales assistant. They both ordered business cards.*

One day, a fax came through with a business card order request. The person's name was listed, and the title read president. The HR assistant was on vacation, so the sales assistant ordered them for her, just to be nice and so the "president" wouldn't have to wait for his order. The cards went directly to the address on the business card, and a week later, the recipient called the HR assistant cracking up laughing. She didn't know what he was talking about or even understand how that could have happened. While he was flattered, he was also somewhat patronizing and asked "How much did that lack of attention to detail impact my bonus?" Once the assistants figured out what happened, they told me, and I told the real president. He wasn't happy with the sales assistant, but she explained she thought that maybe we were doing something new like they did at her last company and hired regional presidents. He appreciated her willingness to help, and the president "wanna-be" was not eligible for his bonus that year, as you had to be in good standing, and needless to say, he wasn't. We also centralized the business-card-ordering process so only the HR assistant would process the orders, as she would know who was hired, their title, etc.

There is a more subtle problem in this situation, too, and it is a political one. When employees believe you are being deceptive because of something you did without consulting anyone first, that produces perceptions of distrust that can carry over to other behaviors and situations. With human resources, despite what the old saying implies, it is always better to take the time to "ask permission first," rather than "beg for forgiveness" later.

Get It in Writing

You can change a lot of things in an organization, but when you start messing with people's pay, they sit up and take notice. As one CEO explained, "It's easy enough to upset people for free, so why mess with their pay?"

Of course, our goal is not to upset people at all if we can help it. However, decisions that managers make are not always well-received, but they are almost never received well when the verbal commitment doesn't match what actually happens. The following story points out that all agreements made between employees and employers should be in writing — no exceptions!

We hired a tradesman at $20/hour to manage the construction of an entire apartment complex. The project manager [PM] verbally agreed to $20/hour with the tradesman. Unfortunately, the PM never submitted any paperwork for the new hire, so the person never got paid.

After three weeks, the tradesman asked how the pay cycle worked — weekly, biweekly, monthly? He was told it was weekly and that the first check took some time to arrive. Another three weeks went by, and because there still wasn't any paperwork, there still wasn't a paycheck.

The tradesman inquired again, and the PM apologized and said he should have his check in a week. Two weeks later, the check finally arrived. The hourly rate was $15/hour. Not only did the poor guy have to wait two months to get paid, but his rate wasn't what had been verbally agreed to.

When he asked the PM, the PM said that because business had slowed down, he was over budget, so all he could afford now was $15/hour. On top of that, because *business was down, the tradesperson wasn't going to be able to find another job. So he stayed, but what a lousy way to do business. I was ashamed to be associated with the company.*

Of course, "get it in writing" seems obvious, but unfortunately, this doesn't happen all the time. A signed document showing the actual agreement can prevent initial relationship and trust problems. And, from a public relations perspective, employees, vendors, and others are less likely to perceive the company as engaging in "a lousy way to do business."

There is, of course, one drawback to getting things in writing — *it's in writing*! Therefore, as stated earlier, we recommend having a second set of eyes proofread your work. Here's one story that was tasteless, at the very least, and caused needless emotional upset for an employee:

It was getting close to the Christmas holiday season, and we had a supervisor who had been off for an extended period due to minor surgery. Up to that point, he had provided only verbal support to confirm that his absence was medically related.

We finally requested, by phone, written medical proof of his surgery and a tentative return date. In return, I received a handwritten note from the employee that stated the dates he went to visit the doctor and his planned date of return. This really upset the HR manager who believed the person was milking the system and abusing our trust.

I was requested by the HR manager to draft a letter requesting the information from a doctor. As these types of letters go, it was the usual request with the added statement that "failure to comply will result in disci-

plinary action up to and including discharge." Since my boss had a sense of humor, I added a final line after the threatening statement, "P.S. ... Have a Happy Holiday!"

Somehow, neither my boss nor his secretary proofread the letter; it was sent to the employee as it was drafted. Upon receipt, the employee immediately called the plant manager, read the threats, and, nearly in tears, added that we sarcastically said, "Have a Happy Holiday"! We did manage to get the information we needed, but I learned that it was not the brightest move on my part.

When we communicate only in written form, the reader cannot see our nonverbal behavior or our true intent and, as such, it poses a risk for misinterpretation. How many of you have written something in an email, for example, that has been taken out of context or has been interpreted differently than you intended it?

As you no doubt already know, what *you* think is funny doesn't always come across that way to others, as this next story pointedly illustrates:

We had a new sales rep coming in from out of town for orientation. Our VP of HR was not a huge fan of this new hire, mainly because of how he acted after the job offer. The VP asked me to prepare the itinerary for his visit. It was customary at our place for all the executives to meet with the new hires, and different people would do the tour, take the person to lunch, dinner, etc.

So, just to be funny, I sent her the itinerary I prepared. I had her picking him up from his hotel, taking him to breakfast, giving him the tour, taking him to lunch, then dinner, and then ultimately back to his room. For every "event," I listed her name. He was expecting the agenda, and he was looking forward to spending time with the executive team. Unfortunately, she forwarded the agenda exactly as I had prepared it.

He immediately called her asking why he wasn't going to be meeting with the other executives. She had no idea what he meant, because she didn't even open my document. She just assumed it was fine! To make matters worse, the president of the company stopped by to see why he wasn't on the candidate's schedule.

Of course, the vice president was remiss here in not opening or checking the document she forwarded. But the HR person is also at fault for using the situation for his or her own purposes — to play a joke on the vice president. This situation resulted in an unwarranted expenditure of time and emotional energy for everyone involved, as well as creating for the newly hired employee an erroneous initial impression that the executive team was disinterested in his successful launch with the company.

The lesson learned by the vice president is a valuable one: read *everything* that goes out with your name on it. And the lesson learned by the HR person is no less valuable: if a joke or prank can backfire, it will!

You've Got Mail!

In the last few years there have been numerous examples of emails that have been the undoing of employees. Whether it has been the inappropriate use of email for soliciting donations or for political purposes, sending highly personal or angry messages, or the general misinterpretation of the language used, organizations are becoming more and more vulnerable to what is bandied back and forth in emails. For example, have you ever sent an email to the wrong person?

The CEO of our company was reporting via email back to his board of directors regarding the status of the open CFO position. The board knew that the controller had applied, and in the emailed report the CEO told the board that the controller was not going to get the role. He added, "I don't even know how long she'll be here." He meant that once she found out she wasn't getting the promotion, she would probably leave.

However, he sent this as "reply all" to an email that the controller was originally copied on. The CEO realized it immediately and called our CIO who, unfortunately, was gone for the day. After not being able to find anyone in the IT department that could retract the email, he called me [the HR manager]. I thought he was going to cry. He asked me if I thought she had read it yet. I looked outside and saw her car in the parking lot, so I told him I figured she had seen it. He asked me what he could do. I told him I thought he should just be truthful and apologetic. I suggested he apologize to her about finding out via an email that she wasn't going to get the job, and then to explain what he meant by the comment regarding how long she'd be there.

He asked me to sit in on the conversation, so I went and got her, and told her the CEO was on the phone and wanted to talk to her. She thought she was going to lose her job, so when he explained the situation, she was actually relieved it wasn't what she had thought. She said she hadn't planned to leave, as she liked it there, and while she was disappointed she didn't get the role, she understood. They joked a bit, and she was ultimately fine with the whole thing. I think the best thing he did was to address it right away and to have me present as a neutral third party.

There are two lessons for us here. First, of course, is the lesson we have reiterated several times already: proofread *every* document before it is sent! However, the second lesson is equally important; in just about every conversation between an employee and an employer, it's best to have a third party present. And, as an HR professional, you are a perfect choice to be that third party. You never want something to be misinterpreted or to become a "he-said, she-said" conversation.

Another common email mistake is sending the wrong information or sending information that should not be shared, as evidenced by this vice president's *faux pas*:

It was the end of a long day, and the VP of Sales was getting ready to send out his sales figures for the quarter. He was pretty proud that he had them completed and wanted to communicate his team's results. So, he wrote a nice note to all the sales managers, highlighting the sales team's achievements, and then he attached what he thought was an Excel report showing the quarterly sales numbers by region.

As soon as he pressed "Send," it hit him. He had just received each sales manager's salary in preparation for their annual merit reviews, which happened to be on an Excel spreadsheet. He frantically went back to double-check his "Sent" file, praying it was the correct document. It wasn't. Instead, he had just sent his entire department's salary information to all the sales managers throughout the company!

He ran to my office. I was opening the document at the same time he approached my office. He was white as a ghost, and said, "What can I do?" I immediately called IT to have them recall the document, but it was too late. Three managers had already opened the document.

While the others were recalled, we quickly visited the three who had seen the document explaining the error and the confidentiality of the information in the file. We had them double-delete the file and asked that they not share what they had just seen. One of the three had only opened the email, but not the attachment, so we were really only dealing with two managers who had seen something they shouldn't have. It could have been much worse if it had been sent during the day when most would have seen the document right away but, luckily, this was sent after hours, so most everyone was already home.

I did have to have several discussions with one of the managers who now wanted his department's employees' salaries increased based on what he saw. While this was very time-consuming, I listened to him and conducted a salary survey for his department so we could both see what the market rates were for his area.

To Disclose or Not to Disclose Pay

The previous story brings up another common subject, which is not so much a mistake as it is a philosophy: should you disclose pay ranges, either to current employees or to candidates? The research on "pay secrecy" is fairly clear that it generally doesn't work the way top managers think it does.

First, because most employees want to know how they compare to others, when pay scales and ranges are not disclosed, employees make erroneous assumptions. Studies have shown, for example, that employees who were asked to estimate the pay of other managers in their organizations tended to overestimate the pay of peer managers and managers that were one level below them, while underestimating the pay of managers one level above them.[1] Moreover, employees in organizations that have pay secrecy tend to perceive the pay system as unfair, whether it really is or not and, as a consequence, are less satisfied with their own pay.

Second, in many organizations that have pay secrecy, the connection between pay and performance is often misperceived. When it is not clear to all employees the level of performance required to achieve a particular level of pay, the result will often be a less motivated workforce. Of course, merely making salary information public will not solve the pay-performance connection. People still need to know what they must do to obtain raises, merit pay, or bonuses.

Third, pay secrecy tends to allow managers to give raises or allocate pay based on favoritism or to avoid difficult discussions. Managers are less apt to overpay favorites or to appease "whiners" if they realize that their pay decisions will be scrutinized by others within the organization. Pay transparency might also help to reduce pay discrimination based on gender, race, or other protected group status.

On a practical level, organizations often believe that it saves time during the selection process by disclosing pay ranges to potential internal and external candidates. To go through an entire selection process, only to find out that the job entails a salary lower than what the candidate expected or would accept, wastes time and resources. Moreover, other interested candidates may no longer be available or, worse, they may have been told that they were no longer in contention for the position.

Pay secrecy is nothing more than a lack of knowledge. But, from an employee's perspective, it also translates for many as a lack of trust on the part of their organization. As an HR professional, you represent the management that is associated with this potential lack of trust. It is in your best interests to foster as much openness, transparency and, therefore, trust as possible. Convincing the top management in your firm to establish equitable pay scales, transparent pay-performance links, and fair pay processes will, in many cases, eliminate the need for pay secrecy policies.

Legal Headaches

One of the most important areas in which human resources needs to "measure twice" is in the area of legal liability. A poll released by the National Federation of Independent Business found that 47 percent of small employers are concerned or very concerned that they will be sued in the next few years.[2]

We've all had nightmares about being sued or have been sued in the past for mistakes that, in retrospect, we can't imagine we didn't catch. Some have to do with missing cues about problematic behaviors of current employees, and some have to do with thinking we have all our "ducks in a row" when it comes to paperwork. Here's a story about the importance of making sure your documentation is correct:

> *Our corporate office began an initiative to do a comprehensive I-9 audit. We went through our current I-9s to update them wherever necessary, adding any that were missing. It took some time (we had 500 employees), and toward the end I heard my assistant laughing. When I asked her what was so funny, she showed me an I-9 from one of the employees in the plant. The one form of ID he provided to the HR person at the time (not me of course!) was a "Social Security card" — with a Hustler magazine ID number and photo to match! I had to go explain to him that his Hustler card wasn't a proper form of ID and that he had to provide another!*

Thank goodness it was an audit initiated by the company and not by Immigration and Customs Enforcement of the Department of Homeland Security. However, some documentation that is given by employees is not always legitimate, but how do you know, and what do you do if your manager says to ignore it?

> *I worked at a distribution company that hired temporary seasonal workers in a primarily Hispanic community. Most of the applicants had poor English skills. However, they didn't need to speak English to do the job. So, as long as they had proper documentation to work in the United States, we could hire them. The HR staff had to decide to accept the ID given to them or to confront them about their ID, knowing they had poor English skills and probably wouldn't understand what was being asked.*

> *When I asked the general manager what he wanted to do, the GM decided that the $50 fine was cheaper to pay if we ever got caught, compared to a recruiter's fee which was typically one-third of someone's starting annual salary in order to find a legitimate worker. So this became a constant ethical dilemma for me and the HR staff. The boss said to violate the law and wanted the staff to gamble that we wouldn't get caught.*

Clearly, the HR professional has a duty to inform the manager. Remember, however, that legal liability extends to you, personally, as well as to the organization. In some states, there are protections for individuals, but many states do not have such protections. Make sure you check with an attorney to see how far the legal liability reaches to individuals before you just accept at face value what your manager tells you he or she is willing to risk.

Helpful Tips

1. Make sure that everything with your name on it is reviewed by you before sending it on to others. That includes letters, contracts, emails, and job offers.

2. Review with top management the policy on whether or when salary information is shared. Giving management the reasons why pay secrecy may undermine motivation can help them understand the issues of perceived vs. real inequity for their employees.

Closing Thoughts

As an HR professional, you role is often as a mediator between two parties that have misunderstood each other or a situation. As such, never take that role lightly. It can be the difference between clear communication and misinterpretation; it can help save a relationship or dissolve one; it can foster trust or create distrust; and, ultimately, it can prevent further problems for you, employees, managers, and the organization overall.

Take the extra time to proofread documents and emails, as well as to double-check your own perceptions and understanding of what is said and meant. It is a small amount of time that is well-spent in the long run.

In other words, "measure twice, cut once." Why waste a perfectly good 2x4?

6 Don't Be Penny-Wise and Pound-Foolish

An estimated 15 percent of the U.S. workforce (19.2 million workers) regularly abuse alcohol.[1] Out of this estimate, 2.3 million workers drink before work, 2.1 million employees work under the influence, and 11.6 million workers come to work with a hangover. Statistics also suggest that more than one-third of Americans over the age of 12 have used marijuana, hallucinogens, cocaine, or other psychotherapeutic drugs for recreational purposes.[2] As you no doubt have already discovered, substance abuse by employees is a real problem. In fact, studies generally find that employees who abuse alcohol and drugs:

- are three times more likely to be involved in an accident;

- are two and a half times more likely to have absences lasting eight days or more;

- use three times the average level of medical benefits;

- are five times as likely to file a workers' compensation claim;

- function at about 67-70 percent of their work potential; and

- are more likely to be involved in theft of company property.[3]

Screening employees who abuse contraband substances is probably already on your to-do list of pre-employment practices. In this chapter we discuss the type of screening that we believe will provide better results than what many of you may already be using. We also provide you with some tools you can use to convince your boss that skimping on drug testing because of initial cost results in being "penny-wise, but pound-foolish."

We Already Do Urinalysis ... Isn't That OK?

Although not every organization has a drug-testing policy for their employees, a large number of organizations now do pre-employment drug testing. Despite our best intentions, however, some tests are better at detecting the presence of contraband substances than others. Of the methods generally used, urinalysis is by far the most widely used testing procedure, as well as the most inexpensive. A variety of techniques is available to test urine for the presence of drugs; however, some are more reliable than others.

For example, thin layer chromatography (TLC) is a technique that is used to separate different molecules that are present in urine. This test (also known as the EMIT test) is not very reliable at all, especially for detection of cocaine, marijuana, PCP, and LSD, and it is extremely labor-intensive for toxicologists to perform.[4] One of the problems with the EMIT test is that no relationship has been demonstrated between the amount of a drug found in the urine and a simultaneous state of drug intoxication.[5] Thus, positive results do not establish when or even whether the drug was used. Positive tests can result for those people who sat in the same car or room as a marijuana smoker, even though they did not use the drug at all. And, of course, tests come back positive when subjects have eaten poppy seeds (since poppies are an opiate) or other derivatives of plants that produce hallucinogenic substances. According to Dr. David Greenblatt, professor at Tufts University Medical Center, "EMIT assays for substances of abuse in urine are of little or no value and should never be used as presumptive or definitive evidence that a person has or has not taken a particular drug."[6]

Approaches to Masking Substance Abuse

Besides giving a lot of false negatives and false positives (i.e., people who test negatively but have used drugs, and people who test positively but haven't used drugs), urinalysis can pose problems because of inappropriate collection and tampering, as the following stories point out.

> *One of our employees violated our company's drug-free policy; his post-accident drug test was positive for marijuana. He was put on suspension and went through a drug counseling program with a certified substance abuse counselor. His counselor finally permitted his return to work as long as he passed a follow-up drug test. So, he took the test, but this time his sample came back positive for cocaine, which meant automatic termination of his employment. The employee came into the office to meet with me to try to keep his job. When I told him that he had a second offense due to the positive test for cocaine, he said "You don't understand. That was not my urine that was tested. I was afraid that I would still be positive for marijuana, so I snuck some of my buddy's urine into the drug test site and poured his urine in the cup instead of mine." I then explained to him that even though it may not have been his urine that was tested, he was still being terminated for tampering with a company drug test. Unfortunately, I could not fire him for stupidity as well!*

***

We had a workplace injury within our company so, following our company's Drug Free Workplace policy, we sent the injured worker for a drug screen. Later that day, I received a call from the testing site stating that the test came back as nonhuman urine. I just had to ask ... was it dog, cat, or alien? Of course, the testing site didn't tell me, but the end result was that the employee was terminated for tampering with the drug-screen evidence.

***

I received a call from the medical review officer for our drug-testing program. He asked if our employee looked different or had been acting strange. I asked him why he would be wondering about this. He said, "According to the temperature of his urine sample at the time of the collection, the employee should be dead!" The temperature of a urine sample should fall within a range that is very similar to one's body temperature. So, this employee either cheated or was dead, because his urine sample had a temperature of 64°F!

In addition to these creative approaches toward urine substitution, there are also a number of products on the market that can mask the presence of drugs in one's urine, sold variously under the names of Absolute Detox XXL drink, Absolute Carbo Drinks, Ready Clean Drug Detox Drink, Fast Flush Capsules, Ready Clean Gel Capsules, as well as others too numerous to mention. These are generally purchased from certain specialty stores, through magazines, or via the Internet. Believe us when we say that the majority of people who use drugs take these products prior to pre-employment substance abuse screening tests!

A referral for a customer service rep came from one of our most valuable associates who recommended her sister. The candidate interviewed well, the manager was pleased with such a quality candidate, and the current associate was excited about the potential of earning a referral bonus.

An offer was extended to the candidate on a Thursday morning. She was told to get a drug test within 48 hours. She said she wasn't able to go on Friday, so she asked if she could wait until Monday. While we don't normally like to have that much time between when we ask for the test and when it's actually taken, we didn't suspect any ulterior motive, as it was the sister of one of our best associates.

However, when the drug test came back positive, I had to call the candidate to inquire if there was something that may have caused a positive result. She said, "You mean other than pot?" I said, "Yes." She said, "No, I tried to take something to mask it, but it obviously didn't work."

I was shocked, but she was more disappointed that she wasted her money on the drug masking product she bought. Out of curiosity, I asked why she smoked the marijuana when she knew she was going to have the drug test. She said, "I thought about that, but it was the weekend, and well, you know ... I thought that detox drink would work."

Some people think that drinking a lot of water or taking vitamin B_3 (Niacin) can also dilute the concentration of drug metabolites in their urine below detectable thresholds. It doesn't. In fact, urine that is too diluted is usually reported as a positive finding for drugs. Fortunately, most reputable drug-testing labs now test for possible adulterants and masking agents in the sample of urine or blood, but they don't catch all of them.

If You Are Going to Screen, You Might as Well Do It Thoroughly!

Hair and saliva specimens are *much* better alternatives to urine and blood for drug testing.[7] Hair generally retains the presence of drug metabolites for up to 90 days. Saliva, while having a substantially lower detection period, is sometimes preferred over hair, because it is not able to be adulterated in any way. In addition, saliva testing is low cost, noninvasive, and is a great choice for organizations that implement random testing programs or post-accident testing on site. Therefore, we strongly recommend both of these methods.

Despite the fact that hair testing is somewhat more costly than urinalysis, the benefits outweigh the greater cost. One benefit is that there is no known effective mask for traces of drugs in hair, primarily because drug metabolites are encased in both the shaft and the follicle of the hair. So, even if someone shaves his head or washes her hair in aloe or another masking substance, a hair follicle may be used instead. Other body hair (e.g., leg, face, chest, pubic area, etc.) can also be used just as effectively. Additionally, because the presence of contraband substances lasts longer in hair, it is less likely that a candidate for employment just "happened to be in the car with someone who smoked dope," or that he or she refrained from taking drugs for a period of time prior to application for employment with your organization. In other words, if you use hair for drug tests, you are likely to catch almost all of the chronic substance abusers!

Random Testing

Far more difficult for HR managers is the issue of random substance abuse testing. Many of us struggle over whether to have such a policy, given the issue of employee privacy. One example of an invasion of privacy tort action featured Simone LeVant — a diver at Stanford University — who won her landmark case.[8] In this situation the judge ruled that an NCAA regulation, requiring that Ms. Levant submit to drug tests prior to a diving meet, constituted an invasion of privacy. One reason for this ruling was the NCAA requirement that Ms. LeVant provide a urine sample in the presence of an observer. However, the following story indicates to what lengths employees will go to "pass" a drug screen, even when someone is right there!

When I was the health resources leader at a Fortune 500 company, an employee came in to provide a urine specimen for a drug test. This test was no surprise, as it is specified in the continued employment agreement. A further stipulation of this agreement is that the test be observed by someone in the same area during the collection process. I, of course, was that person.

The employee began urinating into the specimen container. Suddenly, urine began spraying all over the container, very much like a shower head. The employee became agitated. He set the specimen container down and was making movements like he was adjusting something in his pants. All of a sudden, a false penis and bladder fell into the toilet! This situation, of course, resulted in the termination of this employee. His attempt to adulterate a drug test specimen was regarded in the same way as a positive test result, and he was terminated in accordance with the specifications in his continued employment agreement.

Previous cases that have involved the extraction of bodily fluids have found that the tests themselves must be administered in a way that does not excessively intrude upon the subject. Factors that need to be considered in authorizing tests or procedures must include the extent of intrusion on personal privacy and bodily integrity. Thus, the requirement in the previous story (that the test be observed by someone in the same area) could be disputed by the candidate as excessive intrusion.

It also shouldn't be a surprise that employees try to get out of random testing, even if it means revealing other "skeletons" in their closet:

> *We had random drug testing in place, but we had one employee who, every time he was selected for a random drug screen, had "forgotten" his ID. The hospital needed the employee to have identification to be tested, so we would put his name back in the "hat" and draw someone else's name.*
>
> *After the third time, the light bulb went off. I knew the employee drove to work every day, so I asked him how he could drive without his license. He explained that he got a DUI and it was taken away from him! The bad news here is that he was a forklift driver!*

Make Sure You Do This!

If you have random testing or plan on having a substance abuse testing process for current employees at your organization, there are some things you should make sure you do:

1. Write a substantial and legally defensible random testing policy before you begin your program. In your policy you should specify:

a. Exactly the substances you intend to test for and that are considered contraband. Provide a detailed list of them to all employees. Companies should also spell out what prescription drugs are included in their drug policies.

b. The methods you will use to obtain samples, including specifying how the chain of custody of the sample(s) will be handled. Although many organizations still require an "observer" during urine collection, it is *not* a good idea because of invasion of privacy concerns.

c. What constitutes "under the influence" and "possession" of contraband substances. This should entail specifying the amount of a drug or alcohol that is to be considered the maximum amount allowed to be found in the urine or blood of an employee. This is especially necessary for drugs, since there is no objective standard for determining what levels of drugs impair performance.

d. The consequences for employees for "first" strike and "second" strike (if any). This is particularly crucial, since any policy that is to be implemented must be done consistently. Thus, there should be a set of procedures that must be followed for every employee. Some of the procedural items might include the following:

   i. Validation of the initial test by an independent lab or physician of the employee's choosing;

   ii. Mandatory referral to an in-house or extra-organizational treatment program for the first offense; and

   iii. "Second chance" agreements in which the employee and employer agree that, following treatment, subsequent discovery of drug or alcohol use automatically results in termination — no matter what the situation.

The following story illustrates the importance of communicating what is involved in a "second chance" or "last chance" agreement so that the employee is clear that drug use and abuse is not confined to on-the-job violations, but applies to *all* contraband substances on and off the job:

> *We have a random drug-testing program in our organization. One individual had previously tested positive for marijuana, but was following the necessary guidelines to remain an employee. However, in a follow-up, random drug test the employee again tested positive for marijuana. Our company's policy states that after two "strikes" an individual is to be terminated from his position. In the meeting to discuss this second positive test and his termination, the employee seemed to be completely shocked that he was being let go since he smoked "only on his birthday." He couldn't believe that he couldn't even smoke pot on his birthday and that this was going to be held against him.*

While most courts will uphold the immediate termination of employees who are found to be under the influence of drugs or alcohol while at work, experts on drug abuse strongly suggest that treatment should be the preferred first alternative. There is certainly no legal fault with immediate termination, however, as long as it is enforced consistently and in accordance with company policy.

Helpful Tips

1. Do not disclose the results of drug tests to *anyone* but the employee, assuring confidentiality of the results for either "passing" or "failing" the drug test. This should include other employees, supervisors, prospective employers, administra-

tive agencies, etc. It is imperative that this policy be followed, since disclosure to a third party may result in libel, defamation of character, or other potential litigation. This also magnifies the importance of having drug test results *prior* to the new hire starting, in case the results come back positive, which would lead to immediate termination.

2. Negotiate to include random testing in any collective bargaining contract prior to implementing the testing process. It is clear that many labor-management problems can be dealt with most effectively during negotiation of the bargaining agreement. Issues that should be discussed during contract negotiation include

   a. whether pre-employment testing is a condition of employment;

   b. the means by which the presence of illegal or incapacitating substances are to be discovered (i.e., the type of chemical tests to be used, the ability for the employee to provide independent verification of positive results, search procedures, etc.);

   c. the conditions under which post-employment testing is to be required;

   d. who is responsible for paying for the testing (i.e., the company, the union, or the employee); and

   e. the penalties to be imposed for drug possession and/ or use. These issues, clearly stated within the contract itself, should provide adequate protection against union grievances.[9]

Closing Thoughts

Drug and alcohol abuse costs your organization money. Everybody knows that. What is not well known (or at least widely believed) by top management is how investment in better substance abuse testing methods and procedures will actually save money in the long run.

You can help your organization by putting together a cost/benefit analysis that shows your boss how the costs and benefits of better screening outweigh the costs of poor hires, terminations, wasted training and retraining, accidents and injuries, as well as time spent by you and your managers in dealing with employees that have substance abuse issues.

Table 6.1 is a simple example that can get you started. Notice that even though there is still a cost associated with substance abuse testing and the absences, accidents, and management time that accompany substance abuse in the workplace, with the use of better screening tests the overall cost savings is well worth it.

Figure 6.1

COSTS

Test	Annual # of Tests	Price per Test	# Hired	TOTAL COST
Urinalysis	25	$50	19	$1,250
Hair Sample (H)	25	$100	10	$2,500
Saliva Sample (S)	25	$100	10	$2,500
			Total Cost	**$6,250**

Outcomes (with Urinalysis only)	Cost	Number	TOTAL COST
# Applicants Screened Out	$50	6	$300
# Current Employees Detected	$240,000	8	$1,920,000
# Accidents and Injuries	$180,000	3	$540,000
Mgt time in hrs spent on issue	$120,000	40	$4,800,000
# of Absences Due to Subs. Abuse	$150,000	56	$8,400,000
		Total Cost	**$15,660,300**

Continued on next page

Figure 6.1 (continued)

COSTS

Outcomes (with Hair/Saliva)	Cost	Number	TOTAL COST
# Applicants Screened Out (H)	$100	15	$1,500
# Applicants Screened Out (S)	$100	15	$1,500
# Current Employees Detected	$30,000	1	$30,000
# Accidents and Injuries	$60,000	1	$60,000
Mgt time in hrs spent of issue	$30,000	15	$450,000
# Absences	$75,000	28	$2,100,000
		Total Cost	**$2,643,000**

Note: Assumes each employee's salary @ $30,000; each accident/injury @ $60,000; partial management time @ $2,000 per instance; and each absence @ $3,000.

7 Two's Company, Three's a Crowd

As we stated in Chapter 1, inevitably people will say and do dumb things. Since employees spend more time at work than ever before, many of these dumb things will happen at work, because lines tend to blur the distinction between work and non-work behaviors (i.e., what is appropriate or inappropriate at work). Part of the "blur" involves relationships. In various training sessions conducted across the country, we asked participants the following question: "Have you had, or do you know someone who has had, an office romance?" The majority of people answered a resounding, "Yes!" It has been estimated that roughly half of workers have had at least one office romance.[1]

Proximity Makes the Heart Grow Fonder

Historically, most couples met their significant others while they were in school, in a religious context, or through family friends. In the new millennium, women make up nearly half the workforce, and because employees are spending more time at the office than they used to, more and more people are finding companionship at work. Ironically, since background checks are often done on all employees, the workplace may be one of the safest places to meet someone!

People work many more hours than they did 30 years ago and have less time to go out and socialize. So, it is very "convenient" to connect with someone at work. Dress codes are more casual, and employees are more comfortable and relaxed at work. Sometimes, even flirting is seen as a benefit at work. In the *Elle*/MSNBC.com Office Sex and Romance Survey, a 2002 online poll, one respondent said, "sidelong glances and lustful grins are an added incentive to be at my desk each day."[2] We suppose that is what this fellow hopes he finds at his new job:

> *Toward the end of the interview I asked if the candidate had any questions. "What's the ratio of guys to girls here?" I was a little caught off guard, but thought maybe he wanted to know how diverse we were. Before I could answer, he then asked, "How many are single women? I'm looking for a wife."*

SnagAJob.com, an employment agency for hourly workers, discovered in an online poll with 800 respondents across the U.S., that 72 percent of men and 60 percent of women are infatuated with a co-worker. However, the majority (64 percent) intend to keep it a secret. Surprisingly, men are more likely than women to reveal their feelings to the object of their desire. According to this survey, while 40 percent of men say they would reveal their feelings, only 34 percent of women say they might.[3] In fact, 25 percent of men, more than twice the percentage of women (12 percent), said they had "rated co-workers with terms like 'most datable' or 'best-looking.' "

It is true that many people today get married later in life. In fact, the median age for marriage is rising, with women marrying, on average, when they are 25 years old, and men marrying when they are 27 years old. If they meet in the workplace, they have had time to become friends at work first, see each other under pressure, then decide whether or not to become romantically involved. With all this, plus the continued high rate of extramarital affairs and divorces, it should not come as a surprise that more co-workers are falling in love on the job. A 2009 CareerBuilder.com survey of more than 8,000 U.S. employees found that 40 percent had dated a co-worker.[4] In fact, studies suggest that work is already the No. 1 meeting place in which people find their spouses.[5]

Co-workers are not just hooking up off duty either. It seems that every survey that poses a question about sexual activity on work premises finds some respondents admitting to succumbing to temptation, or just taking a risk for the thrill of it. One respondent described having sex on the desk in his cubicle at 1:00 a.m.: "I said, 'We're crazy. We're going to die if anyone sees us, but we kept on going and that made it incredible.'"[6] In a 2007 Office Romance Survey from Vault.com, 17 percent of respondents admitted to having been caught in a tryst on the job — in the boardroom, the stairwell, the engineering lab, the office kitchen, the boss' office.[7] This result is up from 2006, in which only two percent of those polled had been surprised *in flagrante delicto* at work.

HR — Part of Every Relationship, Whether or Not You Want to Be!

Not surprisingly, we received several stories about sex at work. In one, the employee paged the manager to the restroom, ostensibly to fix a plumbing problem, where the two proceeded to have sex. The female subordinate told her co-worker, joking that she could "get it anytime she wanted it at work, but she couldn't even get it at home if she tried." This co-worker began to notice that there were a *lot* of pages. Amusingly enough, the bigger concern of the co-worker was that she saw the employee as not only getting special treatment from the manager, but also receiving significantly longer breaks and increased time away from actually working that the rest of the employees didn't get. So, she went to human resources to complain.

The HR director had video surveillance put outside the restroom and, sure enough, got evidence that both were entering the restroom at the same time. She started tracking the pages, and eventually confronted both employees. Both denied it, stating that they were just fixing the plumbing. Both were suspended with pay while the situation was investigated. Eventually, the female subordinate broke down and admitted to the office dalliance. She said that the male manager forced her to do it. She said she gave in because she didn't want to lose her job. The male supervisor was now in jeopardy of losing his job; of course, there was more to the story.

The co-worker, however, informed human resources about the number of times the female employee had bragged about having sex in the restroom and that she was the one initiating the pages. When the male manager was faced with this, he did confess, and showed the HR director a gift that the female employee had made for him. His point was that if she were being coerced, she would not have made him a gift. Needless to say, both were fired.

According to the 2007 Vault.com survey on office romance, about four-fifths of romantic relationships are between co-workers, not the stereotypical image of bosses with subordinates.[8] Nor do most of the relationships occur between people who work in adjoining cubicles or offices. However, throw away the stereotypical image of the older male boss chasing the younger female secretary around the desk. It is just as likely today that the boss will be a woman! Same-gender romances are not at all atypical, either. One story we were told had to do with two women who began their sexual relationship in a broom closet at work.

One difficulty for HR managers is in dealing with the inappropriate behaviors and the disruptions that occur when two colleagues are romantically involved. By far, however, the most distressing part for human resources concerning office relationships is when they end in disaster.

Breaking Up Is Hard to Do

You may have already dealt with office romance in your workplace. While they may start out great, eventually many of them are problematic. Usually, the problem starts when cupid's arrow breaks, causing the couple to split up. This may even result in each turning against the other. At the very least, it disrupts the workplace to a great extent and, more importantly, requires intervention by managers and, of course, human resources.

The following story demonstrates this well:

> *Our company purchases iPods in various sizes for service anniversary awards. Because they are for associates across North America, we often need to ship them from our warehouse. One of our Canadian associates ordered an iPod which he claimed never arrived.*
>
> *A year later we received a call from a woman saying she had proof that one of our employees was stealing from the company. She came to our office with a box full of office supplies, CDs, office equipment and ... yup, our iPod, still in the original box, but opened. These are stamped with our company name, so we knew it was ours.*
>
> *Apparently, one of our shipping employees was this woman's ex-boyfriend. He lived with her for a while and had recently left her to live with another woman. He left many personal items at her house including this box of stuff from our company. She felt it was her duty to inform us of his misdeeds. We fired the employee the next day.*

Organizations will differ on how accepting they are of office relationships. Usually, when a company has a no-fraternization policy, it is because of the fear of when (not if) the office relationship deteriorates. According to a CNNMoney.com article, while just under a quarter (22 percent) of these relationships end in a long-term commitment or marriage, the other three-quarters go sour.[9]

Despite the increasing numbers of folks involved in a romantic relationship at work, in a survey by the Society for Human Resource Management (SHRM), a whopping 81 percent of HR professionals said they consider workplace romances dangerous because they could lead to conflict within the organization. In fact, 74 percent said they believed it could present a legal liability.[10]

In the worst-case scenario, accusations of favoritism or retaliation after breakups lead to wrenching lawsuits; however, there is also guilt-by-association if one partner does something wrong or is universally despised; and in milder cases, flirtation and affairs breed damaging gossip. Moreover, romantic liaisons — whether leading to traumatic breakup or blissful marriage — can result in sacrificing one's dignity and, perhaps, even the loss of valued employees.

Helpful Tips

Rather than say "don't do it," consider the following tips:

1. Get Written Consent Agreements for Relationships, also known as "Love Contracts." Bring both parties into your office while the romance is still young. Have them agree to the following:

    a) Indicate that the relationship is welcome, mutual, consensual, and that both parties are willingly in the relationship.

    b) Require that issues between the two will not come into the workplace, but if they do, human resources needs to be notified.

c) Close with stating that if the relationship changes (positively or negatively), each party promises to inform human resources.

Double-check with your attorney, of course, before doing this. However, such a policy allows for everyone to be on the same page regarding an office romance.

If you do decide to forbid "fraternization" at work, make sure that it is applied equally to all relationships, not just romantic ones. In other words, any relationship between any two people that results in unethical, improper, or unprofessional behavior would fall under such a policy. The underlying goal of such a relationship policy is to protect and ensure fair and consistent treatment of employees, to maintain organizational integrity and the ability to achieve organizational goals, and to prevent misuse of information.

Closing Thoughts

Some people feel that office relationships have no place at work; others believe it is the perfect place to meet a potential partner. While some companies and their attorneys want to ban them, most of them realize they cannot prevent workplace romance even if they wanted to. A set of policy guidelines posted on the company intranet won't stamp out workplace relationships, and all the sexual-harassment training in the world won't prevent officemates from becoming bedmates. Unfortunately, some relationships do end badly and, in the office, this can cost employees their jobs, organizations their reputations, and much more.

Instead, why not work with your employees and encourage them to inform HR if an office relationship forms instead of trying to ban something that is most likely going to happen even without your blessing and consent? Executives, and their HR teams, must face the fact that workplace romances are not only here to stay, but they are on the rise. We all can do a better job of managing them to minimize negative consequences.

The flexibility of your organization says a lot about its culture, values, and ethics. A savvy organization is going to work with its employees, not against them. It will provide policies and procedures that fit the needs of the employees, not just outdated policies for the sake of having something in place. If management is open to helping employees meet their needs, the employee will normally go above and beyond for their organization.

8 Learn to Anticipate the Worst-Case Scenario

Generally speaking, if you ask most HR professionals what the least favorite part of their job is, they will tell you it is having to discipline an employee multiple times and, ultimately, terminate their employment. However, there are many things that can be done to make the experience less stressful for you, as well as to minimize the potential backlash from employees who are terminated or laid off.

In this chapter, we'd like to share some stories about good experiences, as well as some not-so-good ones, that are related to terminating someone's employment. As with other chapters, learning from the best practices and the mistakes of others will help you in the future.

Downsizing, Rightsizing, and Fantasizing

While HR has always been right in the thick of terminating employees for performance reasons or inappropriate behavior, in today's volatile economy, it is common for human resource professionals to be just as engaged in organizational restructuring (better known to us all under the euphemisms of "downsizing" or "rightsizing"). Despite your best arguments to the contrary, not all top managers understand the detrimental effect layoffs have on the long-term financial and cultural health of their organizations. Additionally, they mistakenly believe that reducing labor costs will result in a reduction in overall costs. This is a fantasy. The reality is that a reduction in labor costs through downsizing usually results in higher expenses for the organization, and that happens for two primary reasons.

What Are Labor Costs Exactly?

First, it is important to know what makes up the cost of labor. Part of the calculation, of course, involves how much money the organization actually spends to provide employees their wages, salaries, and benefits. Most managers think this is where cost savings can be found if they eliminate positions. However, that is only one part of the equation. The other part involves employee productivity, i.e., how much employees actually produce for that given amount of money. Therefore, true labor costs are calculated as Pay ÷ Productivity.

For employers to lower labor costs they must reduce both pay *and* productivity, or they must increase employee productivity. In other words, an organization can decrease what it spends on employees, but that also entails a decreasing ability to provide goods and services to its customers. Conversely, it can keep employee wages the same and increase the employees' productivity. Which option do you think most organizations really want? Which do you think most organizations really do?

A second reason that cutting labor costs usually does not work in the long term has to do with the old saying, "you get what you pay for." If an organization reduces headcount, the remaining employees generally have to take up the slack in workload, and this reduction generally results in higher costs for overtime or sick time (yes, there is always more absenteeism after a downsizing). In addition, sometimes the organization hires lower-paid workers (maybe part-time or contract employees) with the mistaken idea that they will save the organization money. However, this costs the organization in lost productivity, because these lower-paid, less experienced, and slower workers are usually not as productive as the ones they let go, at least in the short-term. All the way around downsizing is a bad situation, both financially and in terms of decreased morale.

As an HR professional, you can provide helpful information to the top managers in your organization concerning true labor costs and any potential real (or imagined) savings of a reduction in force. If you are in a manufacturing organization, this information may be readily available by employee, by machine, by part made, or by assembly line. In service organizations, such as hospitals, schools, retail stores, social services, or financial services, you may need to choose specific metrics for your industry that would capture productivity. Examples include sales per employee, patient load per nurse, student/teacher ratio, and client volume per employee. These are just examples, and you will probably have other, more relevant measures in your specific organization. Whatever metrics you choose, presenting the actual costs per employee may help your managers see the error in assuming headcount reduction is their only option to reduce labor costs.

When Downsizing Happens Despite Your Best Arguments

You may not always be successful in convincing top managers not to reduce the number of employees. In that case, it is helpful to know how to structure a downsizing event that is credible to all stakeholders, that preserves productivity as much as possible, and that reduces the likelihood for post-downsizing litigation by affected employees. Anticipating the worst case in reducing the number and types of employees will help you prepare them and your organization for a smoother transition.

One of the most important questions to ask your top management team concerns their goals for what they hope the downsizing will accomplish. After identifying the restructuring goals, organizations need to identify the job functions and skills that will be essential in operating the company after the layoffs. The key to a successful downsizing is to use layoffs as part of a larger business plan to penetrate new markets, thereby attracting new customers and generating new revenue streams.

Once the initial goals are set and the process is in place, the next step is to create a committee to decide the layoff criteria. The group should include a representative from every affected part of the organization, as well as representatives from as many protected classes as possible. Before creating the layoff criteria, if the company is unionized, the committee should first look at the Collective Bargaining Agreement to see what criteria have already been established and examine any existing policies that may influence how one should go about implementing the layoffs. If nothing exists or there isn't a union, the committee should create a "multi-factored" system that examines several factors, such as length of service, performance record over a period of time, experience working in various positions, and the employees' transferable skills.

Another role of the committee should be to evaluate selection decisions to see whether individuals in protected classes are disproportionately affected. Finally, the committee should set up an appeals board to hear any employee grievances about the decisions, whether union or not. Following proper layoff procedures will not only help turn the company around, but may also help the company avoid costly litigation and maintain the trust of employees during this difficult period of time.

After 9/11, our company's sales were drastically reduced. We had locations across the country. Although we did everything we could to do more with less, we eventually had to close all of our satellite operations. The goal was to operate out of headquarters. We talked about the most efficient way to do this. We knew we'd have to spend money to send HR to these locations to conduct the downsizing meetings, but it was the right thing to do. So, we gradually closed each office. Morale was down, and the other locations were waiting to hear the news that would impact them. Productivity was shot, so we decided just to communicate our ultimate decision and plan to close each location. We offered stay bonuses, outplacement, and severance packages. Our CFO was able to accrue for these expenses in a different "bucket" of money, allowing us to do the reduction in the right way. We even held a job fair. I called all the employers in each area that I saw were hiring and I told them about our situation. They thought it was a prime opportunity and a free way to get good candidates. They didn't have to advertise. We even allowed on-site interviews on company time and, in the end, everyone who wanted a job found a job. We even offered relocation, as these were good, trained workers. Some decided to go back to school and pursue another career, some retired, but those who wanted to work found jobs. The local news came out to do a story on another local company going out of business, but those they interviewed complimented us on how professionally we handled the situation. We kept everyone in the loop along the way, and we did everything we could to help make the transition as easy as possible. To this day, people will comment on how well they were treated. There truly wasn't the "ill will" you often hear of where people are told to call a toll-free 800 number to hear a special message, only to be told that they're fired and have 30 minutes to leave the building!

The Old "Square Peg—Round Hole" Problem

No matter what the economic situation of your organization, there will be occasions when you must terminate employees because of their behavior. This should not be completely unexpected for employees, particularly if proper disciplinary procedures have been followed. Nevertheless, there are terminations that could have been avoided had better selection, training, or coaching approaches been employed early on in the employee's tenure. Often "for cause" reasons can be anticipated by human resources so that performance-based terminations are reduced.

For both the employer and employee, the occasion of a termination can be an impetus to examine what went wrong in the employment relationship. Maybe the person was not a good fit. If so, the HR practitioner should revisit the entire interview process to determine what went wrong and how to prevent putting a "square peg into a round hole" in the future.

As a first step, consider how your organization identifies the criteria for "success" in the job before you begin the recruitment process. Many companies have their HR professionals write advertisements that are based primarily on objective criteria, like educational attainment or number of years of experience. This is often a mistake, because it tells nothing about what a successful job incumbent needs. A better approach is to sit down with a successful incumbent in the job and to find out why he or she has been a success and what he or she believes are the most crucial characteristics, skills, knowledge, and abilities that are needed in the job. Look at the sample advertisement in Figure 8.1 and think about all the different types of "experienced plant managers" that might apply.

There are several places where applicants might think they meet the criteria but, in reality, they may not. For example, just because one lists a requirement of length of experience or, more generically, just says "experience in X," doesn't mean it was successful experience or that it is the most appropriate experience for the organization with the current opening.

Figure 8.1

Fortune 500 company has an immediate need for an experienced plant manager. This position is accountable for the overall operation of a 24/7 operation including warehouse, production, security, maintenance, quality, safety, budgets, labor relations, and talent management.

REQUIREMENTS: B.S. degree required, Engineering preferred

- 5 - 10 years progressive management experience in a manufacturing environment
- Experience in managing a team of first-line managers + 200 or more associates
- Experience in implementing and sustaining Lean Manufacturing practices
- Experience in operating budgets, capital budgets and P&L
- SAP experience
- Experience in a union manufacturing environment

Now consider Figure 8.2.

Figure 8.2

Fortune 500 company has an immediate need for an experienced plant manager. This position is accountable for the overall operation of a 24/7 operation including warehouse, production, security, maintenance, quality, safety, budgets, labor relations and talent management. We are interested in candidates who have successfully demonstrated competencies in the following:

1. Engineering or a related technical field
2. Strategic and long-range planning, preferably in a large, unionized manufacturing facility
3. Collaborative management with first-line managers
4. Implementing and sustaining Lean Manufacturing practices
5. Financial acumen in preparing operating budgets, capital budgets, and profit-loss statements
6. Understanding and use of enterprise requirement planning software, SAP preferred

---

Notice that this advertisement is much more specific about the competencies required for the successful applicant. All things being equal, a more targeted advertisement, along with appropriate selection measures that test whether an applicant can demonstrate the six competencies listed, will improve your chances of finding the right candidate.

Realistic Job Preview (RJP)

A realistic preview of what the job entails benefits both the candidate and the organization in terms of retention, commitment, and satisfaction. Many organizations try to sell the job candidate on the positive aspects of the job, neglecting to mention the not-so-positive aspects of both the job and the organization. For example, in the 1980s, New York City had a very difficult time retaining city sanitation workers. You can imagine that not everyone is cut out to work in the sewers underneath Gotham. Even though the city raised pay, increased vacation time, and provided other perquisites, many new hires began the job and then quit before their paperwork had even made its way through the city bureaucracy. Desperate to fight the almost 100 percent turnover rate, the city took a camera into the sewers to film "A Day in the Life of a City Sanitation Worker." The camera captured the camaraderie among the workers, the nastiness of the duties associated with the job, the fact that the worker was exposed to extreme weather, and other good and not-so-good parts of the job and working for the city.

As applicants filled out their applications, they watched the short video about the city of New York and about the job itself. Many got up and walked out before finishing the application. However, the ones that stayed understood far better what they were in for if they were hired. Not surprisingly, the turnover rate fell almost by 50 percent after instituting the realistic job preview.

"I've Always Wanted to ..."

In some ways, terminating an employee who doesn't fit the job or the organization does both the employer and the employee a favor. Finding the right fit will be better for both parties in the long run, as the following story indicates:

We had one employee who worked in the Inside Sales Department as an account specialist. She consistently did not meet her performance goals. The manager coached her, and I even talked to her to see if there was anything preventing her from doing her job. She basically didn't feel comfortable asking the customers to purchase more. She said they would come to her with a budget, and she felt good when she could find them a "deal." Instead of suggesting that they use their entire budget or even exceed their budget, she was proud to help them find what they needed and to stay under budget. Her manager told me I had to fire her. While I understood that we couldn't keep her in that role since she wasn't meeting her sales goals, I knew she meant well and was a good employee otherwise.

I approached our customer service [CS] manager, and I explained the situation. I felt like she was good at and enjoyed helping people find what they needed, so I thought a customer service representative [CSR] role would be ideal. When the CS manager approached the sales manager, he told him that I was moving a problem. I felt confident that was not the case. The CS manager trusted me, and we moved the employee to his department. She was a true fit, really liked what she was doing, and was promoted to a team leader in less than one year. In fact, she was asked to provide training for the newly hired incoming associates to both the CS and Inside Sales Departments.

Granted, internal transfers do not always work out for a variety of reasons and, of course, some employees are not good performers no matter where they are placed. Assuming training has been provided, and other avenues have been explored, sometimes the only alternative is to terminate the person's employment.

In some instances, employees may consciously or unconsciously be asking you to fire them. They know, deep down, that employment with your organization just isn't a good fit, but it may be difficult for them to admit it to you or a manager, particularly if they have no other options for a job at the moment. In one of our stories we were told about an employee who asked human resources in his termination meeting why it took so long to reach the decision to let him go. He said he was so bored and unhappy with his current position, pay, and title that he had no reason to stay, except that his wife wouldn't let him quit because he wouldn't get unemployment. Unfortunately, his job performance was not meeting standards, so the company decided to fire him. He was so excited and told the HR representative that he had been dying to quit, and now he'd be getting unemployment while he sat at home looking for a better job. He actually thanked the HR person over and over again.

Depending on the situation, termination opens the door for the employee to do something he always wanted to do. In the 2009 movie, "Up in the Air," George Clooney's character, Ryan, has the unenviable task of terminating scores of people across the country. In one particular case in which Ryan tells an older man that he is being let go, Ryan notices on the man's resume that he went to school to be a chef. He asks the man, "When are you going to get back to your original dream?" Although the man wasn't happy that he was losing his job, he discovered as he sat there that he had put his true vocational dream on hold while he pursued a job that really wasn't his true calling.

As an HR professional, do your homework on what other vocations or organizations might be a better fit for anyone you terminate. It helps ease the awkwardness of termination and provides a more positive ending to the employee's relationship with your company.

The Role of Coaching and Discipline Is to Gain Acceptance, Not Compliance

Terminating someone's employment is the last step in what should be a progression of attempts to help the employee improve. Many managers believe that employees are lazy or that they intentionally perform badly. Most of the time, however, that is not true; employees don't come to work every day trying to do a poor job. Rather, they often are not sure what is truly expected of them or how to reach those expectations. As such, here are some actions you can take to help the employee accept and better understand his job and overall role in your organization:

1. Make sure the employee is clear about performance expectations and any other details that would enable the person to perform effectively. For example, job descriptions, posted production standards, and performance data, such as a 90-day or annual review, helps the employee better understand and perform his role.

2. If the employee is violating policies and procedures, make sure these are written and that the employee has received training on these topics. A signed form is good evidence to reduce the potential for future litigation, especially if a co-worker is doing the training.

3. Make sure the employee is receiving regular feedback about his or her performance and understands the potential consequences of underperformance. Step-by-step coaching allows for improved performance that helps an employee improve his or her work performance. Coaching has been shown to be very effective and can "save" an employee who just didn't understand an aspect of the job or standard of behavior.

4. Examine the performance standards and ensure that you are applying them fairly across the board. All employees who are failing to follow your policies must be disciplined in the same way.

The following story illustrates the pitfalls of having inconsistent standards across the organization:

> *A group of physicians had several offices with different assistants running each one. One doctor would tell his assistant that it was okay for her to wear jeans on Friday. A different doctor told his assistant that she had to follow the dress code and jeans were prohibited. That assistant called HR to find out why she was being discriminated against. While the doctor felt he could do whatever he wanted, it wreaked havoc with the employees of the other doctors. Unfortunately, we couldn't discipline someone else for not following the rule, because the policy wasn't being implemented across the board in the same manner.*

5. If you determine that a performance improvement plan (PIP) might help the employee succeed, use it to positively encourage the employee. A PIP is designed to facilitate constructive discussion between a staff member and his or her supervisor and to clarify the work performance to be improved. The supervisor, with input from the affected employee and advice from human resources, develops the improvement plan; its purpose is to help the employee to attain the desired level of performance. The detail required in a PIP sometimes helps failing employees reach clarity about job expectations.

Specifically, a performance improvement plan should include the following:

- Specific statements and examples of the performance to be improved.

- Specific description of the level and consistency of work performance expected.

- Identification of the support and resources you will provide to assist the employee.

- The plan for providing feedback to the employee, including specifics on frequency of meeting times and persons to be present at those meetings. Specify the measurements you will consider in evaluating progress.

- Specific possible consequences if performance standards are not met.

- Sources of additional information to be used as helpful references, such as the employee handbook.

6. Most importantly, make sure to document any performance discussions for the employee's file with the time, date, and policy or performance problem clearly identified. We even recommend summarizing a verbal warning in writing and dropping it into the employee's file. Minimally, good records will refresh your memory. Employees move on, and good records ensure the employer will be able to address any issues about performance in the future.

As the following story suggests, even the most rudimentary documentation will do:

> *Once, when I was conducting a performance management training session, one manager said that it was ridiculous for us to expect him to carry a pad of paper and a pen around, because he worked in the field and that it just wasn't practical. I asked him if he ever had a tissue or a napkin with him. He said he always had a napkin, as he often needed to wipe his hands. I explained that he could even write notes on a napkin. Everyone started laughing, but I told them that I was serious. The point was to document the situation, the discussion, and the facts. The manager was relieved that he could use whatever was handy, and in fact, he did just that. About*

one month after the training, he came to me with a per-
formance problem. I asked him what had been done to
date. From his pocket he pulled out some napkins with
very detailed notes. He did indeed have sufficient docu-
mentation to proceed with disciplining the employee in
question.

Non-punitive Discipline Is Most Effective

Remember that discipline is not intended as a punishment for an employee; rather, its goal is to assist the employee to overcome performance problems and to satisfy job expectations. Discipline is most successful when it assists an individual to become an effective performing member of the organization.

Non-punitive discipline is a technique that involves the employee accepting responsibility for his or her own choices, as well as becoming accountable for solving the performance or behavior problem. It is likely that many of you have experienced the "dump and run" phenomenon in which an employee "dumps" a problem on you and then "runs" out, only to leave you the responsibility for solving it. Non-punitive discipline turns the performance problem back to the employee to solve. Your role, or a direct supervisor's role, is to help the employee think through options for solving the problem and, if appropriate, provide resources to help him or her proceed to solve it. Generally, the non-punitive discipline process is also progressive in its approach. The recommended approach is as follows:

- Issue an oral reminder that gets the employee to solve the problem himself. For example, if the issue is tardiness, talk with the employee about options he or she can explore, and then get a commitment from the employee to try one of the options for a month. Send a written email or letter to the employee summarizing what was discussed and what the employee committed to do.

- If the employee is still tardy after the month's trial, issue a written reminder and meet privately with the employee. Remind the employee that he or she agreed to solve the problem, and at this meeting, again get commitment to behavioral change. Compose a summary of that meeting and give one copy to the employee and keep one for the file.

- Sometimes, there are still employees who don't solve their performance issue. If the tardiness continues, give a paid "decision-making leave" that forces the employee to decide if he or she wants to stay with the organization. After the one-day leave, set the final consequence if another tardiness occurs. Again, summarize the meeting and the consequences, giving a copy to the employee and keeping one for the file.

- If no further incidents occur over a year's period, the disciplinary documentation is removed from the employee's file. If another incident does occur, then termination is appropriate.

Obviously, the key is to solve the problem, not to punish the employee. The benefit of this process is that it ensures that employment termination is never a surprise. When you schedule the termination meeting, the employee should know what is coming. Also, remember to always have another management witness present when talking to an employee concerning serious discipline.

Termination: The Final Solution

If coaching and non-punitive, progressive discipline do not work and a performance improvement plan did not get the employee back to where he or she needed to be, and you have sufficient documentation, then you are ready to terminate the employment relationship. If that is the case, these are suggested steps to use when you schedule and conduct an employment termination meeting.

Steps for the Termination Meeting

1. Schedule a meeting that includes the employee, the employee's supervisor, and either an HR representative, or in some cases, the supervisor's manager, or even a union representative, if appropriate. We recommend that these meetings be held mid-afternoon on a Tuesday or Wednesday so that the employee has the ability to start a job search immediately and get questions answered before a weekend. Some managers like to wait until Friday and not have to face anyone over the weekend, but this is not recommended. People often go home and after talking to family and/or friends, they have questions. They would prefer to get their questions answered the next day instead of having to wait an entire weekend. The Golden Rule is a good rule of thumb to follow here. If it were you, how would you want it handled?

Our COO came to HR to request a termination meeting. She had all her documentation, and it was with an employee whose role was being eliminated. She said she'd be right there to assist with any questions. When the employee came in, the COO told her that her job was being eliminated and that HR would be going through the details. Then, just as I was beginning, the COO said she had an appointment, grabbed her purse, and excused herself. Flabbergasted, I continued the meeting, but I didn't have most of the answers to the employee's questions, as they were things the COO would typically answer. Later, her assistant told me that the COO grabbed her purse and said she'd be back the following week! However, this experience taught me to ensure the firing manager was going to be there for the entire termination

*meeting, as well as the following day, to answer employ-
ees' questions.*

2. Schedule a follow-up meeting. Emotions are high after this
    initial meeting, and often the employee forgets what was actu-
    ally discussed in the first meeting. Scheduling a meeting for
    the next day in which deadlines, forms, COBRA, and other
    issues can be discussed gives the employee a night to think
    about questions to ask, as well as a clearer mind to ask them
    and remember the information.

3. Follow the termination/severance provisions of your employee
    handbook. Our recommendation is to offer both severance
    and outplacement. If possible, have the outplacement pro-
    vider on-site so that training can begin immediately. We have
    found that such training is helpful for a variety of reasons.
    For example, an outplacement consultant is usually seen as
    a neutral third party. So, if there is a severance agreement
    involved, the outplacement provider can remind employees
    about the importance of not burning bridges and encour-
    age them to sign their agreements. They can also help the
    employee get back on his or her feet more quickly than the
    person could do alone. This will pay off in reduced unemploy-
    ment claims. These professionals have a number of resources
    and connections that can help the person move forward with
    their next opportunity, not to mention assisting them with
    their job-search strategy and revising their resume and cover
    letters. Also, with the severance agreements, employees can
    secure some additional funding now that they are unem-
    ployed, preventing potential lawsuits by offering monetary
    compensation in exchange for a signed release.

During the termination meeting, be straightforward, letting
the employee know he or she is terminated. Give the employee
the real reason for the employment termination, but do it with
compassion.

During my first ever termination meeting, I did it all wrong. I didn't have a witness, and I started with small talk with the employee when she entered my office. I was nervous, so I asked her how she was doing, out of habit. Well, she proceeded to tell me about her three kids and how their dad was a deadbeat and that she was struggling to feed her kids and could barely keep her head above water. Then she asked what it was that I needed. Ugh! I had to tell her that I became aware that she had falsified some company records. She insisted that there must be a mistake. I showed her the paperwork, and then she started to explain the reasoning and how there must be something I could do to give her a second chance. About 15 minutes into the meeting, I told her that she was being fired. She screamed and said that I could have at least told her that upfront instead of acting all phony and nice to her in the beginning. She was right. While it wasn't phony, it sure appeared to be once I finally got to the reason for the meeting.

Know that while employers are free to fire at-will employees for any reason or no reason, there should always be a legitimate reason, because some "bad" reasons can result in liability. If firing the employee violates a fundamental, public policy, or if the employer negligently or intentionally causes the employee some kind of personal injury, the employer may be liable for damages for emotional distress or punitive damages, in addition to being liable for the employee's economic losses.

One employer told his employee that she was being terminated and that in their state, since they were an at-will employer, he didn't have to provide a reason. She had been with the employer for close to eight years, so not only was this hurtful, but she didn't have any closure. She wasn't about to sign the severance agreement, as it appeared to her to be based on age or racial discrimination. Had he given a reason, whether or not she agreed with it, she could have moved on, and it might have all been behind them. However, they are probably both looking at several years of litigation, not to mention bad feelings and public relations.

Remember the simple rule "If you don't have something nice to say, don't say anything at all." If you truly can't think of anything positive, a simple "it isn't working out" will often suffice.

Another employer invited his employee to a conference room. He didn't have the lights on, and there were four executives present when this entry-level employee walked in. He said "pretty ominous" isn't it? She was speechless. She felt intimidated with all the people there, and his comment didn't help. The fact was, he was nervous too, and he didn't know what to say, so he chose something inappropriate. Had they all practiced, he could have had something a little more comforting or appropriate to begin the conversation, such as a simple "Have a seat."

4. Respect the person's dignity. Allow him or her to speak if they want to and ask for any questions. It is best to not engage in much discussion about what went wrong in the employment relationship. The decision has been made, and it is what it is. Never allow the person to think you might be "talked out of" the decision to terminate his or her employment.

5. Always have another management witness present when terminating an employee. The employee may try to "get even," to lash out, or to start accusing others. Don't argue with the employee or try to "settle the score." Recognize going into the meeting that you are likely very disappointed, too. You had an expensive investment in this employee's success, both

personally and financially. You will have to recruit and train the employee's replacement, assuming the person is being replaced. Make sure that *your* emotions are under control!

The department manager and I practiced the termination meeting the day before and the morning of because the manager was so nervous. We each had a script of who was going to say what, in what order, etc. It was planned very well, and it was to be short and concise. I went to the manager's office, and she called in the employee. The employee walked in, and the manager began to cry. Not a word was said, the employee had no idea what was going on. She had a bad feeling since I was there on behalf of HR, but she didn't know for sure. Luckily, I had been through this before, and I even had the manager's script since we had so thoroughly planned out this particular conversation. I jumped in and shared both what the manager was going to say along with my part. The employee was so concerned about the manager who couldn't stop crying, she asked if she was going to be OK. She even said "thank you" and that she understood on her way out.

6. Depending on how the meeting goes, you may want to offer advice to the departing employee. For example, you could mention employment resources. As mentioned earlier with the 2009 movie, "Up in the Air," you could mention their strengths, and perhaps you might offer suggestions of another area to pursue in order to help build the employee's self-esteem and to help them begin the process of job searching. One HR professional shared with us that he had good feedback from former employees that it was so nice to hear something good on their way out. While brief, the discussion helped them clarify their direction and helped them move on.

7. Collect all company property or determine its location. This is when having an inventory comes in handy. It is pretty embarrassing when you have to ask the employee if he or she had a laptop or a cell phone. You should have that information in advance, so you can say, "I'll need to get your laptop and your cell phone."

8. Give the employee a choice about who among the meeting attendees will walk with him or her out of the building, if company policy requires the person to be escorted. If you can have the meeting close to a door that would allow the employee to just leave without having an escort, that is preferable. Also, give the employee a choice about whether he or she wants to remove personal belongings from his or her workstation now, after hours, or to have someone do that for them.

9. Complete all of the steps in the Employment Termination Checklist (see Figure 8.3).

Figure 8.3 Employment Termination Checklist

Specific Questions Which Should Be Asked In Deciding Whether to Discharge an Employee

1. Does management have a legitimate, nondiscriminatory reason for the termination?

2. Does management's documentation support the legitimate, nondiscriminatory reason for the termination?

3. Has the employee threatened with discharge been spoken to in order to get his or her side of the story?

4. Have all other potential witnesses been spoken to?

5. Is the employee being treated in a manner consistent with your employee handbook or other established policies (and have specific rule violations been identified and have disciplinary procedures been followed)?

6. Have the management decision-makers treated any other employee differently who has committed the same offense, particularly with regard to such factors as race, sex, religion, national origin, disability, or other locally protected classes?

7. Has the employee complained of discrimination, harassment or failure to accommodate a disability, and, if so, have such complaints been properly addressed?

8. Does the discharge appear to be in retaliation for any previously filed discrimination claim or charge?

9. Does the discharge violate the National Labor Relations Act or any public policies with regard to such matters as polygraph testing, workers' compensation, or "whistle-blowing"?

10. Are you prepared to communicate the decision to the employee, without overstating or understating the reasons for the termination, and being sure to avoid false, misleading or inconsistent statements by management?

[Figure 8.3 Employment Termination Checklist continued]

Post-Decision Termination Considerations

1. Do you have another management witness present when the decision is communicated?

2. Have you truthfully stated the basis for the decision, without misstating (either overstating or understating) the reasons for terminating the employee?

3. Have you maintained compliance with any applicable wage payment laws, severance policies, administration of benefits, and insurance law requirements?

4. Have you considered providing post-termination benefits in return for a release?

5. Have you treated the discharged employee fairly with regard to all post-termination issues?

6. Do you always give so-called "neutral" references regarding former employees in order to avoid charges of defamation and/or discrimination?

7. Have you counseled supervisors and others who have contact with employees not to violate the company's neutral reference policy so as to avoid liability for both the company and themselves as individuals?

8. Have you considered whether a discharged employee who is in a "protected" class can be replaced by a qualified individual in the same class and at the same salary?

9. Have you carefully reviewed and/or obtained counsel with regard to any proposed responses to inquiries from unemployment compensation agencies so as to maintain consistency with previously stated reasons for the discharge?

No termination checklist can guarantee success in avoiding post-employment lawsuits by disgruntled former employees. Rather, the measures suggested above are recommended as common-sense precautions which should help to minimize an employer's potential liability for post-discharge employee claims while further enabling the employer to maintain good employee relations on the basis that fair-discharge policies and procedures will be consistently followed.

Reprinted by permission of Maurice Baskin, Esq., Partner, Washington D.C., office of Venable LLP. The "Employment Termination Checklist" is available on the ASAE & The Center for Association Leadership web site at www.asaecenter.org/PublicationsResources/whitepaperdetail.cfm?ItemNumber=12216. Retrieved on January 1, 2010.

Occasionally, firing an employee is an immediate necessity for the safety and well-being of the rest of your employees. In such cases, the termination of employment will be immediate. These would be good examples to list in your employee handbook. These often include situations in which an employee:

- threatens violence or commits a violent act;

- brings a weapon to work;

- views pornography on work computers and on work time;

- steals company property; and/or

- commits similar offenses of a dire nature.

In cases such as these, here are some suggested steps to follow:

Immediate Employment Termination for Cause

1. Safety should be your top priority. You need to make sure that the employee is not a danger to himself or herself or other employees.

2. If you suspect he or she is a threat, help other employees to safety and call your security department and/or law enforcement authorities immediately.

3. If the employee does not appear to be dangerous, notify your internal security professionals and/or law enforcement authorities if an illegal act has taken place.

4. Start the meeting by stating the offense calmly and with a witness in the room. Remain polite and respectful. Do not engage in small talk. Instead, tell the employee his or her employment is terminated at the beginning of the conversation.

5. Be sure to obtain all company property. In fact, as stated earlier, you should have a checklist of what has been given to each employee so this will be an easy process and you don't have to ask questions such as "Do you have a laptop or a desktop?"

6. Allow the employee to pack personal items from his workstation with human resources or a manager present, if circumstances warrant and if the employee chooses to do so. As mentioned earlier, it can be very demeaning for someone else to pack up the departing employee's personal belongings, but on the flip side, it can also be very difficult as the "survivors" walk by wondering what is happening. Offering to do this after hours is another viable option, again depending on the situation.

7. Enable the employee to ask any questions about the end of employment and provide answers. If you don't have the

answers, try to find out and call the employee or schedule a follow-up meeting.

8. If the situation warrants it, escort the former employee from the building with the understanding that if he or she returns it is trespassing. Otherwise, let the employee leave on his or her own.

Unfortunately, as we said in the beginning, people will say and do dumb things. Even trained managers will not follow rules, and that's why it's a good idea to have Employment Practices Liability Insurance.

Employment Practices Liability Insurance

We heard about one experience in which an HR professional suggested that the company renew their Employment Practices Liability Insurance (EPLI) to protect against worker claims that their legal rights have been violated. The newly appointed CEO said the insurance was not needed, because the company already had general business liability insurance and the chances of them needing the "extra" coverage were slim.

However, the two types of insurance coverage are quite different. General business liability covers bodily injury claims, personal injury claims, and property damage claims. EPLI covers businesses against claims by workers that their legal rights as employees of the company have been violated. EPLI provides protection against many kinds of employee lawsuits, including sexual harassment claims, discrimination, wrongful termination, breach of employment contract, negligent hiring, failure to employ or promote, wrongful discipline, deprivation of career opportunity, wrongful infliction of emotional distress, and mismanagement of employee benefits plans, among others.

The company in this story had previous sexual harassment claims, several wrongful termination claims, and even deprivation of a career opportunity claim, so it was a prime candidate for such coverage. Unfortunately, the president thought he knew more than the experienced HR person and canceled the coverage, which proved disastrous in the not-too-distant future. Just like with automobile insurance, though it's rare that you'll need it, just in case something happens, you have it. It's always better to be safe than sorry. Interestingly enough, having EPLI coverage can reduce other types of insurance premiums, so instead of being shortsighted, consider protecting your company and its employees with EPLI.

Take Your Purse

A change in leadership at the top sometimes involves a change of leadership throughout the organization, and this might even be you, as the following story recounts:

> *From day one, I knew the new president didn't value HR. He asked me almost as soon as we met, "So, what is it you do again?" He hadn't had an HR department in his previous organization, and he didn't have any interest in having one now. This became even clearer when he asked me to help him to start outsourcing all of the HR functions, and I knew it wouldn't be long before my own job would come into question.*
>
> *Training was the first to go. Then, payroll. The Benefits Department was seen as unnecessary, and the HR group began to dwindle. Even the employment function was outsourced, so I knew it was just a matter of time. When I got the invitation for a meeting via Outlook titled "Miscellaneous Items," I knew. I called my husband to let him know that I was going to be losing my job that day. He told me not to be so negative. But I had lunch with a colleague who told me to "trust my gut." My fear was that I didn't want to have to walk back to my office,*

the furthest one from my boss' office, to get my purse on my "escorted" departure. So, I decided to take my purse with me to the meeting.

When I walked into the meeting after lunch, my boss introduced me to a "consultant" that he had been working with. He told me immediately that he didn't have good news, and as disappointed as I was that my hunch was right, I proudly told him I figured that, which is why I brought my purse. His eyes almost fell out of his head, and he was shocked that I knew. Again, while it was not what I wanted to hear, my anticipation of the worst made the conversation go a lot easier that day, and once we came to an agreement, I simply walked out the door with my purse on my shoulder.

Lower and middle managers are often vulnerable when the organization's top managers change. The rationale for their dismissal may have to do with the worth of the department (as we just saw in the previous story), but it may also have to do with the new management's desire to bring on people he or she has worked with in another organization. There is not much you can do to change this situation, except fall on your sword. However, anticipating a potential change in your situation at work will allow you to have your resume updated and contacts alerted before the ax falls.

Helpful Tips

1. Terminations begin with selection. Make sure that managers really know what they are seeking in a new employee by studying the competencies of a successful incumbent before you begin recruitment.

2. Provide a Realistic Job Preview during selection so that the candidate understands what is expected and has a chance to self-select out of the process.

3. Coaching and performance improvement go hand in hand. The ability to clarify expectations and performance standards, and to show the employee you are invested in their success, will usually work. Make sure line managers are trained in how to successfully coach; otherwise, use an outside expert.

4. Use discipline as a means to gain agreement with the employee of what improvements are needed, not as a means of punishing them. Be mindful that employee punishment never works in the long run and, in fact, may result in worse behavior, such as sabotage, theft, and even violence.

5. Termination is difficult for employees, but it is equally difficult for managers and the HR professional. It is never easy to end a relationship, even when it may not have been the most productive or satisfactory one. If you have done all that you can do in making sure the selection process is valid and that training and coaching were available to help the employee get back on track, then you should have fewer terminations to conduct. But when you must do them, remember that respect and support for the person is just as important as following a set of standard guidelines.

6. Protect yourself and consider purchasing EPLI coverage to keep your company safe and financially solvent.

Closing Thoughts

According to Maurice Baskin,[1] the most common reason that organizations become involved in litigation is due to complaints by former staff and employees who are upset with the way something was handled. Employment-related claims and jury verdicts are increasing, almost to the point of being out of control. When it comes to termination, many of these can be avoided by anticipating the worst-case scenario and making sure your organization has done all it can possibly do to help employees be successful from the beginning.

9   Rome Wasn't Built in a Day

I bet you have probably heard the same statement that we heard at least a hundred times after telling family and friends the things that happen to us on a daily basis at work: "You should write a book!" Well, we decided to do exactly that, and what you have read is a compilation of some of the many stories we received from human resource professionals just like you. While we thought that having some well-needed comic relief was reason enough to write it, we also remembered what our parents told us: "Learn from your mistakes" or, better yet, "Don't do what I did." We thought it made sense to provide tips on how to handle these funny, scary, and peculiar situations. Additionally, we wanted you to know that you are not alone. We are fortunate in human resources, because we have colleagues who are willing to share their experiences and tips to help us. We are all better together. You probably have heard the saying that if everyone threw their problems in a bowl for others to see, you'd probably grab your own issue back? Well, sometimes it just helps us to know that other HR folks have had experiences similar to (or worse than) our own. If we prevent at least some of these things from happening to you in the future, we will have fulfilled what we set out to do with this book.

Review, Revise, Reinvent, and Realize Results

Go back and *review* the helpful tips from each chapter. Use the resources we provide to give you new approaches and new ideas that you may not have tried before. Why re-create the wheel? You may also wish to break each tip into smaller components and devise a plan for yourself and your organization. You could do this by quarters or even months. Choose whatever timeline or strategy works for you.

Once you have reviewed what you are currently doing in some of the areas we discussed, you may want to *revise* some of what you've been doing, particularly if it isn't working the way you would like it to work. For example, if you have a sexual harassment policy or a nepotism policy, no need to do away with them. Instead, consider adding a paragraph about the "love contracts" we discussed. Look at your employee rules and policies and intentionally analyze what behaviors they are reinforcing. If they are rewarding the wrong behavior, revise them so that they accomplish the purpose for which they were created.

As you review, you may find something that actually needs *reinvention*. Perhaps your training approaches have become stale and outdated, or your employees do not feel appropriately appreciated. Don't do a survey! Gather several employees together and talk with them about the issue. Get their honest feedback and suggestions, and then involve them in redesigning the entire program from scratch. It will put new life in all of you.

Finally, take this information and *realize* results. We provided some suggestions for concrete developmental activities in every chapter, and we hope you'll try some of them. We suggest you start with a "Plan to Realize Results," as shown below. Following this template, there are additional suggestions about how to complete a development plan. Here is an example to get you started:

Plan to Realize Results

Directions: Evaluate your current state of performance and goals, prioritize what needs to be done now and in the near future. Start with your high-priority goals. You can focus on your current strengths and use those to enhance your areas for improvement. Be sure to include timelines and set stretch goals, but make sure they're realistic.

Step One to Realize Results:

If I achieve this goal, what are the best things that could happen?

•

•

If I do not achieve this goal, what are the worst things that could happen?

•

•

||||||||||||||||||||||||||||||||||||||||||||||||||||||||||||||||||||||||||||||||||||||||||||||||||||||||||||||||||||||||||||||||||||||||||||||||||

Step Two to Realize Results:

Development activities: Target-completion date:

1)

2)

3)

Barriers to achieving this goal: Strategies to minimize barrier:

•

•

•

•

How will I know that I'm achieving this goal?   Measures:

•

•

•

•

We talked briefly about emotional intelligence earlier. One of the dimensions of EI is our ability to understand ourselves. That is, are we realistic about our strengths and weaknesses, talents and skill sets? Use your Plan to Realize Results to achieve the next level of skills you will need to advance.

Having this type of plan in writing will help you stick to it. In addition, sharing it with your boss and your team will help you gain support from the top managers, as well as your team. You might even have them help you devise the plan. What better way to gain their commitment than to include them in the process?

When the issue is no longer a concern, you will know you've achieved your goal. That is not to say that this goal won't be replaced by a new goal. This is an ongoing process. There are all kinds of creative minds out there. Just when you think you have a solution to all of the problems, a new one arises, and you'll think, "I wonder if that's ever happened to anyone before?" After a few of those, you will be writing our sequel!

In closing, we hope to have given you greater appreciation for human resource challenges. However, the theories, frameworks, ideas, tools, and helpful tips presented in this book are of little value if they are not put into practice. How about it? Will you put it all together and make it happen for yourself, for your department, and for your organization? What will go into your toolkit?

Remember, it takes time. Don't set yourself up for failure by trying to rush through the review, revise, and reinvent process, and give yourself ample time for your own development process. Remember, Rome wasn't built in a day! But the results you achieve will be worth the effort.

Conclusion

As a human resources professional, you are in a most exciting and challenging field. On the one hand, you have far-reaching influence on the well-being of your employees; on the other hand, you represent the management of your organization in its strategies, policies, and goals. At times your job probably seems almost schizophrenic as you try to balance these two responsibilities.

Nevertheless, successful HR practitioners have learned the lessons that allow them to keep this overarching goal in mind: *What is best for the organization in the long term is best for all members of the organization.* We have written this book with that goal in mind, and we sincerely hope that the nine lessons we present will help you to keep it in mind as well:

Lesson #1: Accept That People Will Say (and Do) the Dumbest Things

Lesson #2: Norms Are Important for Leading and Managing Change

Lesson #3: Some Rules Are Meant to Be Broken

Lesson #4: Don't Do What Doesn't Work

Lesson #5: Measure Twice, Cut Once

Lesson #6: Don't Be Penny-Wise and Pound-Foolish

Lesson #7: Two's Company, Three's a Crowd

Lesson #8: Learn to Anticipate the Worst-Case Scenario

Lesson #9: Rome Wasn't Built in a Day

We wish you the best in your chosen profession. In 21st century organizations, having well-managed, motivated employees is one of the most crucial strategic competencies that organizations have. Help your top management realize that competent, trained, and motivated employees are the key to the organization's success. If you can do that, you will have few problems attracting and retaining excellent employees and managers.

Endnotes

Preface

[1] If you have a funny story you'd like to share, we invite you to submit it by going to http://homepages.utoledo.edu/ddwyer and clicking on the "Funny HR Story" button. Complete the online form and hit "submit." That's all there is to it. Who knows? We may write a sequel!

Chapter 1

[1] Mischel, W. (1977). "The interaction of person and situation." In D. Magnusson & N. S. Endler (Eds.), *Personality.*

[2] Palmer, J. K. & Koppes, L. L. (2004). *Investigation of credit history validity at predicting performance and turnover.* Presented at Society for Industrial and Organizational Psychology, Chicago, 2004.

[3] Fair Credit Reporting Act (FCRA), 15 U.S.C. § 1681 *et seq.*

[4] Available at www.ftc.gov/os/statutes/2user.htm. See also Elzey, L., Stubblebine, D., Strickland, B. and Giamboi, J. (2006). "Criminal Background Checks: A Checklist of the Pros and Cons." www.shrm.org/Research/Articles/Articles/Pages/CMS_000379. aspx. Retrieved May 29, 2009.

[5] www.intelius.com.

[6] www.ussearch.com.

[7] www.careerbuilder.com.

[8] Salovey, P. & Mayer, J. (1990). *Emotional Intelligence. Imagination, Cognition and Personality*, 9, 185-211.

[9] Wechsler, David (1939). *The measurement of adult intelligence.* Baltimore: Williams & Wilkins. Recently revised in 2008 and distributed by Pearson Learning.

[10] To see a list of possible instruments, visit our free resource site at http://northcoasthrllc.com/resources.html.

[11] http://hrinterviewguide.com.

Chapter 2

[1] Excerpted from "Final Say," column by Brian McGrory, May 16, 2007, in the *Boston Globe*.

[2] Backhaus, K. & Tikoo, S. (2004). "Conceptualizing and researching employer branding." *Career Development International*, 9, 501-517.

[3] You can read some of these at http://twitter.com/zappos.

[4] To see samples, visit http://jobsinpods.com.

[5] Wilkins, A. (1984). "The creation of company cultures: The role of stories and human resource systems." *Human Resource Management*, Vol. 23 Issue 1, 41-60.

[6] http://northcoasthrllc.com/resources.html.

Chapter 3

[1] Moyers, B. and Campbell, J. *The Power of Myth* (1988). Betty Sue Flowers (ed.). New York: Doubleday.

[2] Eric Schansberg, "marriage as covenant vs. contract," SchansBlog, October 23, 2007. Available at http://schansblog.blogspot.com/2007_10_01_archive.html.

[3] This analysis, developed by Rudolph Flesch and John Kincaid in 1948, assesses the readability level of a document.

[4] "Tribune Employee Handbook — Must Read!" FishbowlLA/MediaBistro, January 16, 2008. Available at www.mediabistro.com/fishbowlLA/newspapers/tribune_employee_handbook_must_read_75153.asp.

[5] From an editorial appearing in the *San Francisco Examiner*, May 30, 2009.

[6] Retrieved from Careerbuilder.com, January 5, 2010.

[7] Retrieved from http://madtbone.tripod.com/work.htm, January 5, 2010.

[8] Retrieved from www.cch.com/Press/News/2004/2041007h.asp, January 10, 2010.

[9] www.Inc.com November 17, 2004.

[10] Shaw, Bernard (1903). *Man and Superman: Maxims for Revolutionists*. Cambridge, MA: The University Press.

[11] As quoted in *Business Education World*, Vol. 15 (1935), p. 172

Chapter 4

[1] Barrington, L., Franco, L., and Gibbons, J. *I Can't Get No ... Job Satisfaction, That Is*. The Conference Board, Report No. R-1459-09-RR, January 2010.

[2] Kalev, A., Dobbin, F. and Kelly, E. (2006). "Best Practices or Best Guesses? Assessing the Efficacy of Corporate Affirmative Action and Diversity Policies." *American Sociological Review*, v. 71, 4, 589-617.

[3] Catlette, B. and Hadden, R. (2000). *Contented Cows Give Better Milk: The Plain Truth About Employee Relations and Your Bottom Line*. Contented Cow Partners.

[4] Caudron, S. (2002). "Just Say No to Training Fads." *BNET Training and Development*, Retrieved from FindArticles.com, January 30, 2010. http://findarticles.com/p/articles/mi_m0MNT/is_6_56/ai_89149223/.

Chapter 5

[1] Lawler, Edward E., III. "Secrecy About Management Compensation: Are There Hidden Costs?," *Organizational Behavior and Human Performance*, Vol. 2 (1967), 182-189.

[2] NFIB Research Foundation, *2002 National Small Business Poll*. Retrieved from http://www.411sbfacts.com/sbpoll.php?POLLID=0031, February 3, 2010.

Chapter 6

[1] Frone, M. R. 2006. "Prevalence and distribution of alcohol use and impairment in the workplace: A U.S. National Survey." *Journal of Studies on Alcohol,* 67, 147-156.

[2] Dennenberg, T. S., and Dennenberg, R. V. (1983). *Alcohol and Drugs: Issues in the Workplace.* Washington, D.C.: Bureau of National Affairs.

[3] Rohan, T. M. (1982). "Pushers on the payroll: A nightmare for management." *Industry Week,* February 8, 52-57.

[4] Hartsfield, W. E. (1987). *Investigating Employees: A Guide for Employers and Employees.* New York: Callaghan and Co.

[5] Dennenberg, T. S., and Dennenberg, R. V. (1983). *Alcohol and Drugs: Issues in the Workplace.* Washington, D.C.: Bureau of National Affairs.

[6] See Wilson, C. W. (1986). "From AIDS to Z: A Primer for Legal Issues Concerning AIDS, Drugs and Alcohol in the Workplace." *The Labor Lawyer,* 2(4), 631-674.

[7] Kintz, Pascal (2006). *Analytical and Practical Aspects of Drug Testing in Hair,* CRC Press.

[8] See *Hill v. Nat'l Collegiate Athletic Ass'n*, 865 P.2d 633 (Cal. 1994). Note that Simone LeVant had graduated making her participation in the case moot.

[9] Arbitrated decisions have upheld the employer's right to test for drugs and alcohol when (a) company policies are clearly stated, (b) those policies have been communicated to employees, and (c) those policies have been consistently enforced in the past. See Wilson, C. W. (1986). "From AIDS to Z: A Primer for Legal Issues Concerning AIDS, Drugs and Alcohol in the Workplace." *The Labor Lawyer,* 2(4), 631-674.

Chapter 7

[1] *Elle*/MSNBC.com Office Sex and Romance Survey, 2002.

[2] conference-board.org. *The Conference Board Review* Article: "Office Romance: Are the rules changing?" by Janet Lever.

[3] Retrieved from www.snag-a-job.com on November 22, 2009.

[4] Careerbuilder.com, Retrieved February 3, 2010, from www.
careerbuilder.com/share/aboutus/pressreleasesdetail.
aspx?id=pr481&sd=2/10/2009&ed=12/31/2009&cbRecursi-
onCnt=1&cbsid=c1a7373571734ff087eeed89878dc1f3-
318530677-w1-6&ns_siteid=ns_us_g_2009_careerbuilder.com.

[5] conference-board.org. *The Conference Board Review* Article: "Office
Romance: Are the rules changing?" by Janet Lever. Retrieved
February 10, 2010, from http://www.conference-board.org/ar-
ticles/atb_article.cfm?id=344.

[6] Ibid.

[7] *Elle*/MSNBC.com Office Sex and Romance Survey, 2002.

[8] Ibid.

[9] CNNMoney.com article. "Cupid at work: 3 tips for office romances"
by Anne Fisher. Retrieved February 3, 2010, from http://money.
cnn.com/2007/02/12/news/economy/cupid.fortune/index.htm.

[10] SHRM Survey on Office Romance, January 2006. Retrieved February 3, 2010, from www.shrm.org/Research/SurveyFindings/Ar-
ticles/Pages/Workplace_20Romance_20Survey.aspx.

Chapter 8

[1] Baskin, M. (2002). Retrieved from ASAE and the Center for Association Leadership website, www.asaecenter.org/PublicationsRe-
sources/whitepaperdetail.cfm?ItemNumber=12216, January 1,
2010.

Index

About the Authors

Dale J. Dwyer, Ph.D., PHR, is professor of management and former chairman of the Department of Management at the University of Toledo. He teaches and conducts research in various management areas, including human resource management; planning, selection & recruitment; compensation; performance management; and HR strategy and metrics. He is the faculty adviser to the SHRM student chapter.

Sheri A. Caldwell, Ph.D., SPHR is an HR consultant and the former vice president for human resources at Hickory Farms and director of human resources at the Toledo Zoo. She is an adjunct professor at the University of Toledo, teaching organizational dynamics; human resource management; training and evaluation; and organizational leadership. She is the co-author of *Using Your Emotional Intelligence to Develop Others*.

Additional SHRM-Published Books

539 Ready to Adapt Human Resource Letters, Memos, Procedures, Practices, Forms...and More: The Comprehensive, All-in-One HR Operating Guide
By R.J. Landry

101 Sample Write-Ups for Documenting Employee Performance Problems: A Guide to Progressive Discipline & Termination
By Paul Falcone

Assessing External Job Candidates
By Jean M. Phillips and Stanley M. Gully

Assessing Internal Job Candidates
By Jean M. Phillips and Stanley M. Gully

The Cultural Fit Factor: Creating an Employment Brand That Attracts, Retains, and Repels the Right Employees
By Lizz Pellet

Employment Termination Source Book
By Wendy Bliss and Gene Thornton

The EQ Interview: Finding Employees with High Emotional Intelligence
By Adele B. Lynn

The Essential Guide to Federal Employment Laws
By Lisa Guerin and Amy DelPo

The Essential Guide to Workplace Investigations: How to Handle Employee Complaints & Problems
By Lisa Guerin

Hiring Source Book
By Catherine D. Fyock

HR Competencies: Mastery at the Intersection of People and Business
By Dave Ulrich, Wayne Brockbank, Dani Johnson, Kurt Sandholtz, and Jon Younger

Human Resource Essentials: Your Guide to Starting and Running the HR Function
By Lin Grensing-Pophal

Leading with Your Heart: Diversity and *Ganas* for Inspired Inclusion
By Cari M. Dominguez and Jude Sotherlund

The Legal Context of Staffing
By Jean M. Phillips and Stanley M. Gully

The Manager's Guide to HR: Hiring, Firing, Performance Evaluations, Documentation, Benefits, and Everything Else You Need to Know
By Max Muller

Never Get Lost Again: Navigating Your HR Career
By Nancy E. Glube and Phyllis G. Hartman

Performance Appraisal Source Book
By Mike Deblieux

Smart Policies for Workplace Technologies: Email, Blogs, Cell Phones and More
By Lisa Guerin

Staffing Forecasting and Planning
By Jean M. Phillips and Stanley M. Gully

Staffing to Support Business Strategy
By Jean M. Phillips and Stanley M. Gully

Stop Bullying at Work: Strategies and Tools for HR and Legal Professionals
By Teresa A. Daniel